THE
TAMILIAN ANTIQUARY

GLIMPSES
OF
ANCIENT DRAVIDIANS

THE
TAMILIAN ANTIQUARY

GLIMPSES
OF
ANCIENT DRAVIDIANS

BY

MR. E.S.W. SENATHI RAJA LL. B.

EDITOR
PANDIT D. SAVARIROYAN

VOL - I

NO - V

GYAN

Published by

Gyan Publishing House
5, Ansari Road
Daryaganj, New Delhi-110002
Phone: 011-47034999, 9811692060
E-mail: books@gyanbooks.com

Distribution Network
gyanbooks.com
India, USA, Canada, UK, Australia, France

ISBN : 978-81-212-3059-9 (PB)
First Published, London, 1909

2nd Impression 2020

Printed at: Gyan Press, Delhi.

The
Tamilian Antiquary Vol. I No. V
Editor: Pandit D. Savariroyan; Mr. E.S.W. Senathi Raja

THE TAMILIAN ANTIQUARY
Vol I No. 5
CONTENTS

EDITED BY
PANDIT D. SAVARIROYAN
PUBLISHED BY THE HONY SECRETARY
T.A. SOCIETY
1909

GLIMPSES

OF

Ancient Dravidians

BY

MR. E. S. W. SENATHI RAJA, LL. B.

THE object of this paper is not to air any pretention on my part to shed the light of my researches on so obscure a subject of study as the Ancient Dravidians, but to stimulate original enquiry among the members of the rising generation in regard to local history. There is perhaps no ancient and civilised people whose early history is enveloped in such impenetrable darkness or so inextricably mixed up with mythological legends as that of the Hindu. The spirit of credulity which held us bound hand and foot for centuries and which made us accept without reserve the most absurd and childish fables as genuine and indisputable facts of history is slowly passing away. Until the chains which ignorance and credulity has forged shall be broken off, until we learn to discard as unworthy of credit all accounts traditional or otherwise which cannot stand the test of criticism, and begin to investigate the facts of history as a judge in our courts would scrutinize the evidence in a case, we can make no substantial progress. When once a student starts in the path of genuine historical inquiry or research, nothing can be more fascinating than the study of the history and antiquity of one's own country or race. "Who are the Ancient Dravidians," it may be asked, "and why should we interest ourselves in them?" These are very pertinent questions, and I shall proceed to answer them at once. The ancient Dravidians

A reprint from the Malabar Quarterly Review.

are said to be a race of people whe were the direct ancestors of the Tamils, the Malayalis, the Telugus and the Canarese and some other tribes now occupying the greater part of the southern-half of India from the Vindhya mountain and the river Nerbhuda comprising also the elevated plateau of the Dekhan with its bordering mountain ranges and its narrow coasts. What proof is there, it may be inquired, that the Tamils, the Malayalis, the Telugus and the Canarese have common ancestry? The evidence is partly ethnological and partly philological, that is to say, it is derived mainly from Physical characteristics, customs, manners, habits, tradition and speech. It was the comparative study of the different languages now spoken in India that has revealed the fact that the people now inhabiting India are ethnically of different origin. It is now generally admitted that all the languages of India, may be classified philologically as either Aryan or Dravidian, with the exception of a few such as the uncultivated dialects of the Kols, the Mundas, the Sabaras and other rude tribes of northern India, whose orgin, in the present state of our knowledge, may be said to be unknown. The following twelve languages, spoken by nearly forty millions of people are said to have a common origin viz., Tamil, Malayalam, Telugu, Canarese, Tulu, Coorg, Gond, Toda, Kotta, Rajamahal, Uraon and Brahui. Of these, it is interesting to note, that the last mentioned language, Brahui, is the speech of a people living in Beluchistan. It is to the ancestors of the people now speaking the above twelve languages the name Dravidian has been given, and it is to them that I refer when speaking of the ancient Dravidians.

To understand aright the import of this lecture, it will be useful to take a brief retrospective view of the ancient history of India as brought to light by modern investigations. Who the ancient aborigines of India were, and where they came from, it is impossible to tell now with any degree of certainty. In the rugged mountain ranges and impenetrable forests of Northern India, beyond the Vindhya range, are found the scattered remains of certain wild tribes of a dark colour but not of Ethiopian features. Too little is known of their languages to indicate with certainty whether they are the remnants of the earliest races that inhabited the whole of India at one time; but a comparison of their language with the Dravidian dialects has shown that they are not of Dravidian origin. All that we know for certain is that at the very dawn of history, more than two thousand years before the brith of Christ, these two races were in full possession of India. It is now generally believed, as the result chiefly of a comparative study of languages, that the Dravidians were a fair people. branch of the Scythian family, who had immigrated into India through the North-Western Passes and had probably intermixed with the aborigines.* But these two races were not, however, destined to remain undisturbed possessors of the soil for long. For there poured in again through the North-Western Passes, the gate-way of India, a fresh race of conquerors called the Aryas, who were thereafter to play an important part in the destinies of India. The Aryan tribes who had a common origin with the Persian, Greek, Roman, Teuton and Celt were, like all the successive hordes of the conquerors of Hindustan delighted with the beauty of the country displacing the original inhabitants, and either reducing them to subjection or driving them to the mountain fastnesses. They brought with them their own divirities, religion, institutions and a new language, the most ancient form of the Sanskrit. An imperishable record of their manners, language and institutions are preserved, in the hymns of the Rig Veda. But it was only the northern-half of India however, which they reduced under their complete dominion in the course of many centuries and called it Aryavartha—the Land of the Aryas. Their expansive force was, as a matter of course, exhausted in subjugating the various tribes who preceded them in the occupation of Aryavartha between the Indus and the Ganges. To the South, however, of the Vindhya mountains and the river Nerbhuda, the ancient Dravidians maintained their ground and perpetuated their language. There is no historical or traditional account of any hostile invasion or conquest of Southern India by the Aryans. But the Aryans had, however developed already a high degree of civilization, as may be gathered from their philosophies, their civil institutions, their arts, and their sciences. The Brahminical class had already surrounded themselves with high privileges, as the authorised exponents of religion, as the intermediaries between the Gods and their worshippers and as the possessors of sorcery, witchcraft, charms, incantations and all the dreaded occult sciences. The Dravidian tribes were gradually brought to know and accept, chiefly by the influence of Brahmin pilgrims or adventurers who travelled southward, the Aryan civilization and to adopt their religion and polity. The intercourse between the Aryans and the Dravidians appears to have been always of a peaceful character. The Mahabaratha and Manu, two of the highest and most ancient authorities, represent the Dravidians as Kshathryas who had fallen from their original rank by the neglect of Aryan religious rites. This was evidently, a mistake made by the early Aryans who came into contact with the Dravidians. At the time when the Brahmin ascetics and pilgrims first

---

*[The old theory of Drs. Caldwell and Maxmuller and others of their school that the Dravidian race belongs to a supposed Scythian family and they entered India through the North-Western Passes is now generally considered as not resting on sufficient data. Vide Pandit D. Savariroyan's article "The Bharata Land" pp. 9-18. in the Tamilian Antiquary No. 1. Ed.]

visited the south, it had become an acknowledged practice in Aryavartha, that the first three castes, being Dwijas or Twice-Born, should wear the sacred-thread and observe the other rites and ceremonies peculiar to the Aryans. But wearing thread was unknown in those days even among the Dravidians of the highest class. Even the ancient Pandiya, Chola or Chera kings do not appear to have adopted that practice. It was purely an Aryan custom and so were the Srartha and other ceremonies which were peculiarly Aryan and were utterly meaningless to the Dravidians of old, as they now would be to the Chinese, Japanese or Europeans. But the northern visitors finding that in the south even kings, princes and nobles did not wear the sacred thread, and that they never performed those household rites and ceremonies which were indispensable to every Aryan, and as their knowledge of human kind had been confined to Aryavartha only, they naturally came to the conclusion that the upper classes in Southern India were degraded Kshathriyas and the middle classes were Sudras, for Sudras alone were not entitled to wear the thread or perform the prescribed household ceremonies in the land of the Aryas. In this connection, I may mention parenthetically that the name 'Sudras' as applied to the Malayalis in Malabar, to the Vellalas in the Tamil country, to the Naidoos among the Telugus and the Komaties among the Canarese is evidently a misnomer; for from the most ancient times these classes were in their respective countries the highest among the Dravidians as well as the principal land-owning caste, and there is no proof that they were at any time slaves of any superior caste, as the Sudras in the north of India were.

In Ceylon the Sinhalese Kingdom of Annuradhapura was founded by Wijayo about the Sixth Century B. C. The land-owning classes there are called Villalas or Goigama and they are considered the highest caste. For 2500 years, under the native Kings, Ministers of State and Governors of Provinces and even the Buddhist priests have been chosen from that caste. It would be as absurd to call them Sudras as it would be to call a member of the English Aristocracy by that name. The fact is the fourfold division of Brahma, Kshatriya, Vaisya and Sudra was purely an Aryan classification which has no application whatever to the Dravidians. The truth of this statement may be easily verified by questioning an ordinary illiterate Tamilian or Telugu or Canarese. If you ask him to which of the four varnas of Brahma, Kshathrya, Vaisya, Sudra he belongs, he will probably stare at you with a vacant look. But if you ask him what his caste is, he will at once reply that he is a Naikan or Vellalan or Shanan or Parayan or some other caste—a fact which conclusively proves a state of things which has existed among the Dravidians from time immemorial viz., that caste system among them was a local one based purely on occupation, and had no reference whatever to the four varnas of the Aryas. By degrees all India became aryanised that is to say, all over India the customs, beliefs, and institutions of the various races were either recast or adapted on the model of the Aryas —a process which is still going on among the lower castes in different parts of South India and even in Ceylon.

There are, however, indications that some of the Dravidian races had attained a considerable degree of civilization, independent of Aryan influences, and it is with them that we are concerned at present. That was especially the case with the ancient Tamil Kingdoms of Chera, Chola, and Pandiya, for they seem to have carried on maritime commerce with foreign nations like the Phœnicians as early as 1000 B. C. As pointed out by Dr. Caldwell, among the articles of merchandise that were taken to Solomon, King of the Hebrews, from Tarshish of Ophir, is mentioned "Tuke" which is the old Tamil word for peacock. The Ramayana, which refers to the invasion of Ceylon by Rama in pre-historic times, refers to the ancient Tamil Kingdoms of Chera, Chola. Pandiya as civilized countries—a circumstance from which one inference at least may be drawn with certainty viz., that whatever may be the date of Rama (that is, if he ever lived), at the time of Valmeeki, the author of Ramayana, those kingdoms were known to be civilized countries. The earliest period to which the existence of Dravidian Kingdoms is traced in historical records is to be found in the Mahavanso, a chronicle compiled by the Buddhist monks who were first sent over to Ceylon as missionaries by Emperor Asoka about 300 years before Christ The Mahavanso uniformly refers to the Tamils of Pandiyan country, as possessing a national existence and civilization anterior to those of the Sinhalese, and mentions that Wijayo, the first king of Ceylon, married the daughter of a Pandiyan about the 6th century B. C. The fact of the Pandiyan kingdom figuring as a well-established monarchy at that period argues to its having been in existence for some centuries at least previously. In the time of Buddha (6th Century B. C.) the principal Dravidian countries appear to have been on a par with those of the north in point of moral and material progress. Megasthenes, the Ambassador of Selecus Nikator, at the court of Pataliputhra in Northern India in the 4th century B. C., could not have heard of the kingdom of Pandiya in the extreme south, if it had not attained considerable power and reputation in his days. The Mahabhashya of Patanjali, which is said by competent scholars to have been composed in the second or third century B. C., speaks familiarly not only of the Pandiya and the Chola countries, but also of particular towns and rivers in the south as Kanchi and Kaveri. The kingdoms of Pandiya, Chola and Kerala are also met with in the inscriptions of Asoka in the third century B. C. The fragments of Eusebius allude to two embassies sent by Pandiyan to Emperor Augustus at Rome, and Strabo mentions that Chera, another Dravidian Prince, sought also the friendship of the Romans. Large quantities of Roman coins dating from the time of Emperor Augustus to that of Emperor Zeno (B. C. 27 to A. D. 491), found in Madura and in several towns on the Malabar coast confirm the accounts of Greek and Roman writers, that trade between Rome and South India was in a flourishing condition from the first century B. C. to the 5th century A. D. Pliny speaks of the kingdom of Pandiya in about 77 A. D. and its capital Madura. Ptolemy in the second century A. D. and the Periplus of Arrian in the third century A. D., refer to the three Tamil kingdoms as prominent in the south. Indeed Porus in the North and Pandiyan in the South seem to have been the two most powerful monarchs in India, whose fame overshadowed the rest in the time of the Greek Supremacy in Western Asia, under the successors of the satraps of Alexander-the-Great. Varaha-Mihira, the great Astronomer who composed his work in 404 A. D., makes allusion to the kingdoms of Pandiya, Chera, Kerala, Karnataka, Kalinga and Andhra all of which were Dravidian, and to the rivers Kaveri and Thamraparni in the South. According to the Chinese authorities, in A. D. 500 an ambassador Leam Woo came from South India to China, who gave them to understand that large trade was caried on between Southern India and the Roman Empire. Before the 5th or the 6th century there appear to have emigrated to Java, Cambodia and Annam large colonies of Dravidian settlers, and there are to be found, even at the present day in the kingdom of Annam and the island of Java, ruins of temples of the 5th and the 6th centuries. The testimony of the Greek and Roman writers attest that Kolkai, the ancient sea-port of the kingdom of Pandiya, was a great emporium of commerce. It is clear, therefore, that at least from a thousand years before Christ, down to the 5th century after Christ, there had been commercial intercourse between the Dravidian kingdoms of South India on the one hand, and the Phœnicians, the Greeks, the Romans, the Chinese, the Arabs, and other foreign nations on the other and that the Dravidians had attained a high degree of civilization independently of the Aryas.

But what was the earliest known condition of the Dravidians before they came in contact with the Aryans? Do we know anything about the beginning of their civilization? Have we any records from which we can gather some glimpses at least of the ancient primitive Dravidians? If we are to look for any such record we must search for it in the ancient Tamil literature which is the earliest cultivated of all Dravidian languages and the great store-house of Dravidian antiquities. It is a well-known fact that the earliest records of all nations are preserved in their national poetry. Of all races of India, the only people, who had a poetical literature independant of Sanskrit which has survived to this day, are the Tamils. The metres and rules of versification of Tamil poetry are radically different from those of Sanskrit. While the sister Dravidian languages, Telugu and Canarese and even Malayalam, have literally borrowed almost all the varieties of Gana chandas and Matra chandas from Sanskrit, the Tamil has alone preserved her ancient metres of Agaval, Venba, Kalippa and Vanchippa. The Arya, Vaitaty, Anustub, Gayatri and other ordinary Sanskrit metres have not their corresponding equivalents in Tamil and are incomprehensible to it, while they are closely imitated by the Telugu and the Canarese poets. The ancient Tamil versification is purely Dravidian, and its genius is utterly distinct from that of Sanskrit. The possession of numerous, varied, and polished forms of verse, independent of any Sanskrit model leads one to the inevitable conclusion that the Tamil branch of the Dravidians had a literature of its own before its contact with Sanskrit. Without a poetic literature metres and rules of versification are meaningless. If that literature had come into being only after Agastya and his disciples had come to the south, it would be a mere imitation of Sanskrit in form and substance, as it is in Telugu and Canarese. Agastya can be said to be the father of Tamil (as it is asserted traditionally) in one sense only; *he was the first probably to introduce a grammatical system founded on a Sanskrit prototype.* It was in all likehood an adaptation from the Rig Veda Pratisakhyas or from some Sanskrit school of Grammarians just as Tolkappiam. the oldest Tamil Grammar extant, is avowedly based on the Aindra Vyakarana. Before the time of Agastya there was an alphabetical system and a literature, as may be gathered from the evidence furnished by the language itself.

The age of Agastya was in reality a new era in the history of Tamil Literature. It was then that Sanskrit influences first began to be felt. Northern religions and social institutions were introduced, and the Brahminical priesthood and in its train the Buddhist, the Nigranthas, the Ajwakas and other religious sects began to pour upon the south. It was then that Grammars, modelled on those of the vedic schools, were first propounded by Agastya and his followers. It was then that literature exclusively Dravidian was replaced by northern traditions and legends. The national literature was slowly modified, its legends transformed, its heroes amalgamated with or lost in the personality of those of the north, and its Gods absorbed with a change of name into the Aryan pantheon. This process of gradual change and assimilation was a *fait accompli* before the 2nd century A. D. for in Ptolemy and the Periplus of the Red Sea the most Southern point of India is known by its Sanskrit name of Kumari.

But some remnants of the old Tamil Literature, which have come down to us, have preserved, it seems to me, some vestiges of the Dravidian society in pre-aryan times, that is at least a thousand years before Christ. The Tamil Grammarians from the time of Agastya and Tolkappiyan have incorporated into their grammatical treatises composed on Sanskrit models, a portion of the old Dravidian literature called *Porul* which does not properly fall within the scope of Grammar in general. *Porul,* literally meaning a thing or object, was in this case limited in its application to two out of the whole range of physical objects or objects of human pursuit that could interest the intellect or exercise the imagination of a people. They were Love and War. The reason of this, to us curious, designation will be obvious, when we look at the condition of the society which invented the term. Turn wherever we may, in a primitive society, love and war were the two things or objects pre-eminently so called, to which all others were subordinated. They alone were the two themes capable of arousing the enthusiasm of the poet, or the strains of a bard. Accordingly we find the earliest Grammarians like Tolkappiyan whose works were avowedly founded on Sanskrit models including a chapter on *Porul* in their Grammars, a chapter which has no place in purely Sanskrit Grammars*. The truth seems to be that *Porul*

*[The assertion that the Grammar Tol-kappiam is composed on the models of Sanskrit grammars is, we fear, resting on insufficient data. We dare say not only the section *porul-iyal* in Tol-kappiam, as the learned writer thinks, but every part of that treatise is undoubtedly independent of Sanskrit. There is no trace of Sanskrit influence in Tol-kappiam and it is quite an independent work. The development of the Southern Clasical Language and its Grammar are *ab-intra.* Perhaps the writer has based his conclusions on the authority of the editorial preface of the work. It is true Panampâranâr, in his preface, states that the Grammar Tol-kappiam is modelled on the principles of *Aindiram.* We doubt much whether *Aindiram* was a foreign element or an indigenous treatise on grammar. The Grammarian Tol-kappian nowhere tells us on what model he composed his grammar. There is no mention by the author of *Aindiram* or *Agathiam.* He has neither told us anywhere that Agathiyar was his Guru nor he owes anything to him as his disciple. But references from Tol-kappiam only go to prove that then existed not only an amount of literature in Tamil but also grammatical treatises before its composition. For we see that most of the rules are concluded in the work by such phrases as என்ப, "they say," என்மனார் புலவர், "the learned thus say," இயல்புணர்ந்தோர் மொழிப, "the Grammarians say so," etc. etc. Ed.]

was of purely Dravidian origin and the Grammarians finding that there was already an ancient literature on the subject which was popular with the poets thought it proper to devote a chapter to that subject in their grammars. It is clear therefore that before *Agastyam* and *Tolkappiyam* were composed there existed in Tamil a literature on *Porul,* for the Grammarians could not have evolved it out of their inner consciousness if it did not exist in their language. Now *Porul* is divided into two parts viz., *Aga-porul* and *Purá-porul* literally meaning internal object and external object respectively. The sum and substance of the former is Love, and that of the latter, War.

Now *Porul* being the oldest fragment of Dravidian Literature which has come down to us from pre-aryan times, a study of its contents must necessarily give us a glimpse into the condition of Dravidian society in those early times. *Aga-porul* treats, as stated above, of love and is conventionally divided into three heads of which the first, though introduced incidentally to play a subordinate part to the third, is, it seems to me, of the utmost importance historically, as furnishing an insight into the condition of Dravidian society in pre-aryan times. The most notable points we gather from it are the absence of caste and of organized kingdoms with crowned kings. There were five different communities scattered in various parts of the country and living apart by clans, each having its own tutelary deities and chiefs, and following its own customs and manner of living. With the introduction of Aryan Gods, the names of some of the indigenous deities were gradually replaced at least in poetical composition by those of the Vedic, an innovation which was naturally to be expected. Those communities of pre-aryan times were as follows:—(1) *Maruta-màkkal* or agricultural tribes. (2) *Kurinchi-màkkal* or semi-agricultural tribes. (3) *Mullai-màkkal* or pastoral tribes. (4) *Neidal-màkkal* or fishing tribes and (5) *pàlai-màkkal* or hunting tribes.

1. The Mâruta-mâkkal or agricultural tribes. They consisted of Uḷavar (Plough-men) who inhabited fertile and well-watered spots, *Maruta-nilam*, so called from the *Maruta* trees (*termmalia alata*) which flourish in the vicinity of water. Their tutelary deity lost his local name and was merged in the personality of the Vedic Indra. They lived upon rice white and red which they cultivated, and drank the water of the rivers which ran past their fields. Their occupation consisted of ploughing, sowing, reaping, and celebrating festivals. On festive occasions and in marching to war they beat a drum called *Parai*. I may here state that the ancestors of the *Paraiar* (Pariahs) of the present day, the beaters of *Parai* (drum) which is still their occupation in North Ceylon, were originally the slaves of the agricultural tribes, and their chief occupation from the remotest times seems to have been beating the drum. In patriarchal and martial times in the pre-historic age they beat the war-drum of the agricultural tribes, but at the present day they discharge the same function more peaceably on festive occasions (மணப்பறை) and on funerals (பிணப் பறை). The Maruta-mâkkal had also a kind of stringed instrument called Maruta-yâl on which they sang a tribal air called *Marutam*. Their towns were called *ûr*, Pêrûr (big village) and Mûdûr (old village). It is curious to observe that the termination *ûr* added to villages and towns is met with in all agricultural districts from the Ganges to Cape Comorin, thus showing that the Dravidian Colonies existed in olden times so far north as the Ganges. Among the *Brahui*, a Dravidian race, now inhabiting Beluchistan, the word *ûr* is employed to mean a house. The chiefs of the agricultural tribes in ancient times were called *Uran* (lord of the village) or *Kiḷavan* (elder, owner). I may here point out that the word Kiḷavan seems to throw some light on the origin of the Pandiya dynasty. The words *Kilavan* and *Pandiyan* are in Cen-Tamil synonymous terms and at first meant an old man or an elder. It has been observed that when nomad communities settle down to agriculture the old men who were before burdens to their descendants became their acknowledged heads

and begin to exercise at first a patriarchal authority over them. With the increase of family this power augments and he becomes a chieftain. The first of the Pandiyans appears to have been precisely one of those patriarchs of an agricultural community as his name seems to imply, who perhaps by conquering some of the adjoining tribes had become a Sovereign. This seems to be confirmed by tradition, which describes the first of the Pandiyans as a Vellala, the principal land-owner caste in all Dravidian countries. It was, no doubt, the first Aryan adventurers from the North, who, finding an apparent similitude of names, traced some connection between the Pandavas of the North and the Pandiyans of the South and assigned the latter to the Lunar dynasty (Chandra Vamsa)* while converting the Mûdûr of the Pandiyans into Madura, by a supposed connection with the Aryans.

2. The Kurinchi-Mâkkal or semi-agricultural tribes. They lived in hilly districts called Kurinchi, a name derived from the *Kuruch* trees which abound in rugged hilly districts. The name *Kuravar*, by which they were known, has been preserved to this day, being applied indiscriminately to mountaineers, foresters, snake-charmers and other backward tribes living in the hills. The tracts of land which they inhabited abounded in forests of the odoriferous sandal-wood, in which roamed ferocious tigers, bears, and wild elephants, and which were thronged with swarms of beautiful peacocks and parrots. They fed upon bamboo rice and millet which alone their barren tracts were capable of yielding, as well as honey and yams which they collected from the forest, and they drank the pure waters of the mountain streams. Their tribal air was a melodious one called *pan* which they sang to the accompaniment of a flute. They marched to battle to the sound of a drum called *Tondagam* and their chiefs were called *Verpan* or *Chilampan* and the common people were also called

---

*[Mr. V. J. Thamby Pillai of Colombo gives other interpretations. *Vide* his article on the "Modern Representatives of Solar and Lunar Races," Tamilian Antiquary No. 1. Ed.]

Iravular (இறவுளர்). Their towns were but modest clusters of huts appropriately styled *Siru-kudi* (little huts) *Kurichi* (குறிச்சி). The termination *Kudi* (குடி), it is to be remarked, has survived to our day in the names of small towns and villages, Tutukudi (Tuticorin) தூற்றுக்குடி, Panakudi (பணைக்குடி, and the word *Kurichi* (குறிச்சி) is to this day used in North Ceylon for a village*. They worshipped a mountain God who was subsequently identified with Skanda. Caivism, under the form of worshipping Civa or Skanda, seems to have been originally the religion of the primitive mountain tribes of India long before the arrival of the Aryas. Kailasa, the abode of Civa, is said to be somewhere above the Himalaya Mountains. Parvathy, the consort of Civa, is represented in the Puranas as the daughter of the king of the Himalayas. The God Civa himself is represented as a beautiful person, with fair complexion, his body smeared with ashes, with locks of hair on his head (from which the Ganges takes its rise) and as riding on a bull. It is said that among the mountaineers of Nepal and other Himalayan districts, the bull is the favourite animal for riding even at the present day. Many of the mountains and hills in India and Ceylon are sacred to Skanda. The worship of Skanda appears to have prevailed in Ceylon very early, for the *Mahavanso*, the Buddhist chronicle of Ceylon, refers to the famous temple of Skanda at Kathirgama in the mountain district of Ceylon, to which pilgrims flock in large numbers from various parts of India and Ceylon even at the present day, as having existed previous to the introduction of Buddhism into Ceylon, 300 years before Christ.

3. The Mullai-mâkkal or pastoral tribes. They inhabited jungle tracts of land and worshipped a deity who corresponded

---

* The ending *Kurichi* (குறிச்சி) appears in the names of such villages as Kalladakurichi (கல்லடக்குறிசசி), Alwarkurichi (ஆழ்வார்குறிச்சி), Chenkalakurichi (செங்களக்குறிச்சி) &c., in the Tinnevelly District, and Kannakurichi (கன்னக் சறிச்சி), Manavalakurichi (மணவாளக்குறிச்சி), Villikuri (chi) வில்லிகுறி(ச்சி) &c., in Travancore. It is even used as a proper name by itself for a village near Palamcottah in Tinnevelly and for another village near Suchindram in Travancore.

to Krishna. Perhaps Krishna himself was originally a local deity as may be inferred from his dark complexion who was subsequently aryanised as an Avathara of Vishnu. Their land was the abode of stags, hares and wild fowls on which they fed, as well as on the produce of their cattle and grains which they obtained by exchange. Grappling with bulls, dancing hand in hand with young cow-herdesses on luxuriant meadows, where their cattle grazed and playing on their flutes their tribal air called *sadâri*, such were the favourite pastimes of the youthful cowherds. They lived in villages called *chêri* (சேரி) and *pâdi* (பாடி) (from *pâdu* to sing) so named perhaps from the clamorous songs and joyous sounds in which their inhabitants delighted, in addition to their bucolic sports. The words *pâdi* and *chêri* again are preserved to this day in the names of many towns and villages in the Dravidian countries, such as Vaniyampadi (வாணியம்பாடி) and Puducheri (புதுச்சேரி). Their tribal drum was called *pambai*. The men were called Ayar and Idaiyar.

4. The Neital-mâkkal or fishing tribes. They lived along the sea-coast in small fishing villages called *pattanam* or *pâkkam*. Their occupation consisted in fishing, fish-curing and salt-making, and fish entered largely into their consumption. They paid adoration to a God who was the Dravidian counter-part of Varuna. They made use of a drum similar to that of the pastoral tribes called *Meenkôl* and played a flute called *Vilari*. Their chiefs were called *Chêrpan* or *Pulamban Turaivan* and *Konkan*, and the ordinary men were called Parathar (பரதர்) and Nulaiyar (நுளையர்).

Here we find an interesting account of the history of the word *pattanam* now generally anglicized into *pattam*. Originally applied to small fishing-villages, it is now used to designate only large towns and cities such as Cennapattanam (Madras). This is evidently from the circumstance that fishing-villages generally rose to importance by maritime commerce and they often attained the proportion of large cities. It is also to be observed that to this day it is only towns on the sea-coast that have the word *pattanam* or *pattam* affixed to their names, as for instance Nagapattanam (Nagapatam), Vizagapatam, Muslipatam, while towns in the interior have the word *ûr* affixed to their names, such as Tanjavur (Tanjour), Chittur, Karur, thus preserving the history of their origin, the former as villages founded by fishing tribes, the latter by agriculturists. It seems also extremely probable that all the towns on the sea-coast bearing the termination of pattanam or pattam and all the cities in the interior with the particle Ur (written also *oor, ore*) affixed to their names, were originally the seats of Dravidian colonies. The antiquity of the term *Ur* is attested by Greek Geographers who refer to *Karur, Thellur,* and other towns in South India. The other term *Pâkkam* employed to denote fishing villages, remains also in use to the present day, but is limited in its application only to comparatively small towns, such as Purasai-pakkam, Nunkan-pakkam, &c.

The word Chêrppan, by which the chiefs of the fishing villages were known reminds us of the old titles of Pandiyans, Kumari-Cherpan (the Cherpan of Kumari). The title must have evidently been assumed by one of the Pandiyans after his conquest of the coast Kumari (modern Cape Comorin) from its maritime chiefs, as the title of Prince of Wales was assumed by the heirs-apparent to the Kings of England, after the conquest of Wales.

5. The Pâlai-màkkal or nomads. They inhabited desert tracts and forests, having eagles, doves and kites as neighbours, and lived on hunting and plundering the adjoining countries. They were called ferocious Vêdar, and they chased tigers with the help of a species of wild dog which they trained for that purpose. Their chiefs were *Kâlai* and they worshiped the Goddess Kàli. Their habitations were called *Kurumbu,* their martial air *pancuram* and their war-drum *tudi.* The people were also called Maravar (மறவர்) and Eyinar (எயினர்).

This class was no doubt the historical ancestors of the Kallar, the Maravar and other tribes, and were identical with the nomads Sorai of Ptolemy, *Sorar* being the old Tamil word for plunderers. They also appear to have been known by the name *Kurumber*, Kurumbu being the name of their villages. According to Ptolemy, the River Kaveri flowed through the land of the Sorai and Arcot was their capital. The names of their original abode are preserved to this day in such names as Kurumbakonam (modern Kumbakonam), Kumbakottai, &c. Tondamandalam, of which the ancient capital was Kanchi (modern Conjiveram), is said to have been conquered from the Nomadic tribes by a Chola general called Adondai (after whose name it was thence-forward called Tondaimandalam) who appears to have divided the land among various clans of Vellalar. The name Kanchi already occurs in Patanjali, and some of the names of places given to them by the Vellala colonists are to be seen in Ptolemy's tables. Kanchi afterwards became the capital of the celebrated Pallava dynasty to which are attributed the works of Amaravathi and Mahamallapura.

It is a very curious fact that as all the ancient institutions of India became fossilized in course of time, the five different tribes above enumerated, have continued to exist side by side for centuries, some of them even to the present day, with their characteristic habits and manners. There are even now living in certain localities people called Kallar (thieves) and Maravar, descendants of old nomads, and Kuravar or mountaineers, plying their old trade whenever it is possible.

That these tribes existed long before Tamil, Malayalam, Telugu and Canarese separated from the common parent-stock and became differentiated into distinct dialects is evident from the fact, that among the Canarese and the Telugus the same tribes exist, bearing almost the same names, following the same occupations and having the same characteristics as those in the Tamil Country. In a very interesting publication called the Ethnographical Survey of Mysore, the author, Mr. Nanjundayya, M. A., M. L., the present

Chief Justice of Mysore, gives the names of some of the above tribes as existing castes in Mysore.

This is what he says of the caste called Koravas or Kurachas, corresponding to the hill-men (Kuruchi-Mâkkal) or Kuravar in Tamil. "Mythology apart, they are a wandering tribe found all over the State. That they are decidedly of Tamil origin is borne out by the language they speak, which is common to them irrespective of the place they live in, whether as Rrukulas in the Telugu country, as Kuravas in the Tamil tracts, as Koramas or Korachas in the Kannada parts or as Korairs or Kaikans in the Maharatta country. ....They speak a language which appears to be a dialect of Tamil or a medley of Tamil, Telugu and Kannada, the first element preponderating.........Korama and Koracha both seem to be derived from the word Kuru, meaning to divine or prognosticate, and are applied to the caste on account of their profession of fortune-telling which their women practise. Some derive these terms from a word which means a hill-man (of Tamil Kurinj:hill country) showing that these are a wild tribe living in jungles." Of the tribe called Beders, in Tamil Vedar (the Pálai-Mákkal of *Agapporul*) he writes "The Bedas called Boyi in Telugu and Vedan in Tamil number according to the latest Census 244,990 comprising 123,345 Males and 121,645 females......As some of the names of the caste unmistakably indicate, the *Bedas* were originally a wild tribe living in jungles and mountains and supporting themselves by hunting. They used to infest the high-ways for robbery and were considered fit instrument for all acts of rapine and cruelty......Their early habits well fitted them for the army of which in later times, they became a most important element. They were largely employed in the rank and file of the armies of Vijianagar Empire. They gradually spread to the South and by the time of Hyder Ali they not only constituted the pick of his army but many of the caste had set themselves up as petty chiefs known as Paleyagars (Polygars Anglice) who had also men of the same caste in their armies.........They seem to be originally a

Telgu-speaking people but after long settlement, those of the Kannada Districts, have adopted that language as their mother-tongue." Of the Holeyas, Tamil Pariahs or Pulayas and Malayalam Pulayas, he writes "The Holeyas numbering about five and a half lakhs and forming a tenth of the total population, are found all over the State of Mysore......These are an outcaste race, Pariah and Mala being their appellation in Tamil and Telugu." The following extract from the Mysore Census Report of 1891 shows that the members of this caste were originally slaves of the land-owning classes. "In most of the properties of Malnad or hilly taluks each proprietor of landed estate owns a set of servants (of the Holeya caste) called Huttalu and Mannalu. The former is the hereditary servitor of the family born in servitude and performing agricultural work for his land-holder from father to son. The Mannalu is a serf attached to the soil and changes hands with it." These instances are, I think, sufficient to show that the five tribes mentioned in the *Agapporul* lived in all the Dravidian countries of the South from time immemorial.

The *Pura-porul* which treats of the external object or war gives us an idea of the political organization of the earliest Dravidians. The different tribes or clans were under the patriarchal rule of their chiefs, who had fortified places and armies. The arms of the soldiers consisted of bows and arrows, swords, and javelins. The chiefs marched to battle to the sound of the tribal drums and flutes and the standard-bearers carried the flags or banners of the respective tribes each of whom had a distinct banner. The soldiers had long hair which they tied into a knot on their heads and they wore anklets on their ankles which made a jingling sound when they marched to battle. I may here observe parenthetically that wearing long hair on the head tied into a knot called Kondai (கொண்டை) as is now done by the Malayalis, and the Sinhalese, was an ancient Dravidian custom and the warriors are described as wearing different varieties of flowers on their *Kondai*, when going to or returning victorious from the field of battle. The Sinhalese, among whom the custom is in vogue at the present day, had evidently copied it from their neighbours the Tamils with many other customs and habits and even elements of cilization as will be found on a careful study of the Sinhalese antiquities. The imitation seems to have taken place very early; for Agathomenis, a Greek Geographer of the 2nd Century A. D., describes the Sinhalese as cherishing their hair like women. The Sinhalese word used for the knot of hair on the head namely *Kondai*, is manifiestly borrowed from the Tamil.

In the *Pura-poul* eight stages are mentioned as characterising wars of those days. 1. The prelude, and indeed the pretext for war in those days, seems to have been the seizing and carrying away by force the enemy's cattle. This was properly the declaration of war. The victor in a sortie of this kind was entitled to certain military honours, and was crowned by his chieftain with a garland of the flower called *Vedchi* (வெட்சி). 2. The aggrieved party then was bound to decide the dispute by the arbitrament of war and marches against the enemy and invades his territory. Warriors who in an attempt of this nature successfully attack the enemy receive the honour of being crowned witha garland of *Vanchi*(வஞ்சி)flowers. 3. The next stage is resistance, and those who offered a valiant resistance to an invading army were decorated with a garland of *Kanchi* (காஞ்சி) flowers. 4. Next the enemy's fortress was attacked by the invading enemy. Those who distinguished themselves in defending a fortress were entitled to the honour of wearing garlands of *Nochi* (நொச்சி). 5. Then follows battle in the open field when the besieged are forced to fight by necessity. Those who were foremost in courting danger in the battle were adorned with a garland of *Thumbai* (Phlomus indica. 6. The victors in the battle who put the enemy to rout and gained complete victory were adorned with garlands of Vagai (Mimosaflexuosa-வாகை). 7. The warriors who vindicated the honour of their tribe and their chief by recovering the cattle that had been carried away by violence were crowned with garlands of *Karanda* or sweet basil (கரந்தை). 8. Victory, however brilliant, will not be decisive unless the enemy is rendered powerless. So the last step was taking possession of the fortified places of the enemy. The warriors who succeeded in these exploits were crowned with garlands of Ulignai (Illicbrum lanatum-உழிஞை). I need hardly say that the state of society which we infer from the above carries us back to remote times, to the beginnings of Dravidian society, to a semi-agricultural and nomadic state when the chief wealth of a tribe consists of cattle. It depicts the state of society at a period when Tamil, Telugu and Canarese had not yet differentiated themselves into separate languages, probably not less than a thousand years before Christ, for in the time of Buddha, the 6th century B. C., Chera, Chola, Pandiya, Andhra, and Kalinga had become organized Kingdoms. Before the time of Buddha, Aryan influences had partly penetrated into Southern India. The age of Agastiya was anterior to that of Buddha. When Agastiya composed his Grammar in Tamil, he and after him his successors in-corporated into their treatises a chapter on *Porul,* which formed the subject-matter of the literature of the poets and bards that preceded him. But as the state of Society portrayed in *Porul* describes the manners and customs of a people who had lived at a period anterior to the formation of the Pandiyan Kingdom itself, I think there is no impropriety in my dating it as early as 1000 B. C. Probably exception will be taken to my chronology by some native cholars, for in the opinion of the late Rai Bahadur Tamotharan Pillai, the Tamil Academy at Madura lasted nearly 10,000 years. The first Sangam lasted through the reigns of 81 Pandiyas, from காய்சினவழுதி to கடுங்கோன். The second Sangam continued to exist through the reigns of 59 Pandyas, from வெண்டேர்ச்செழியன் to முடத்திருமாறன். The last Sangam extended through the reigns of 49 Pandiyas, from முடத்திரு மாறன் to உக்கிரப்பெருவழுதி. Mr. Nagam Ayya, the author of that most valuable compilation the *Travancore State Manual,* says that the Malabar was founded nearly 6,500 years ago.

"Hindu scholars incline to the belief that the Vedic Aryans, must have had a wonderful era of peace and security from foreign agression for about 5000 years before the invasion of India by Alexander of Macedon. This gives a period of about 7600 years to the first Aryan colonisation in the North-west of India. It appears to me that Western Scholars often err in their calculations about Hindu dates relying solely on copper-plate documents and stone inscriptions as if the peopling of a kingdom went only *pari passu* with such symbols of later civilisation as copper-plates or stone inscriptions. If we note the marvellous progress in the colonisation of America since its discovery by Columbus in 1492 A. D. which period of 400 years is only a speck of time according to all known calculations of Hindu chronologists and if we also note how quickly population has pressed and squeezed itself within the last half a century into all available nooks and corners of India in the mad desire to possess land, making one fear that one's grand-childern may scarcely have elbow-room to stand upon, it is not a bold statement to make that within a thousand years after the first Aryan set his foot in the Panjab the whole continent from the Himalaya to the Cape must have been more or less peopled. The fact has nothing to do with the dates when the oldest Indian Epics were written or the feats of Rama and Krishna recorded therein took place. I would therefore give Kerala an age of about 6500 years at least, an inference which should incline one to greater belief in the oral tradition extant than in the learned deductions of scholars."

I do not, however, see my way to accept the above chronologies as historical dicta until they are supported by further evidence.

E. S. W. SENATHI RAJA, LL. B.

THE

AUGUSTAN AGE

OF

Tamil Literature.

BY

Mr. S. Krishnaswamy Aiyengar, M.A., M.R.A.S.

DREARY as the prospect may well appear to the earnest student of Tamil literary history, as in fact does early South Indian history in general, there has, of late, been brought to light a considerable body of Tamil literature which throws a flood of light upon the much-doubted, though often debated, period when literary activity in Tamil reached its high water-mark. Scholars are much divided in opinion as to the Sangam having ever existed at all, except in the active imagination of later poets and the idle tongue of tradition. This is not strange, considering how much truth is generally overgrown and interwoven with fable and legend. Whether wantonly or otherwise, the truth is very often hidden almost beyond recognition in later literature; and early scholars in modern Indian research have unwittingly contributed their own quota to the very same end. Much has, therefore, even to be unlearnt before making an attempt to learn something about this distant past of the oldest of the Dravidian languages of South India. Even in the traditions handed down to us, much distorted though they are, there are certain cardinal facts and characters standing clearly marked out from the rubbish outgrowths. It will not, therefore, be without interest

*A Reprint from the Indian Antiquary, Bombay.

to attempt to place these facts in the light in which they appear, on an unbiassed and impartial enquiry.

An attempt will, therefore, be made in this paper **to set forth the available evidence**, literary and historical, which tend **towards the following conclusions:**—

a. That there was an age of great literary activity in Tamil to warrant the existence of a body like **the traditional Sangam.**

b. That the period of the greatest Sangam activity was the age when **Chenguttuvan Chera** was a prominent character in politics.

c. That this age of Chenguttuvan was **the second century of the Christian era.**

d. That these conclusions are in accordance with what is known of the later history of South India.

There are a number of works in Tamil literature of a semi-historcial character of a later and of an earlier time; and these alone will be relied upon here, without altogether eschewing tradition of a reliable character, as the sequel will amply shew. So far as tradition is concerned, there had been three Tamil Sangams* that flourished at or about Madura, and of these the third is all that we can presume to speak about. This Sangam had for its members 49 critics and poets who constituted a board of censors. There were 49 Pandya rulers among whom were **Mudathirumaran** and **Ugra-Peruvaludhi** who actively patronised the Sangam. This last personage is the sovereign before whom **the Kural of Tiruvalluvar** received the Sangam imprimatur. It is not out of place to remark here that the author of the *Kural* was not among the Sangam members, and there were a large number like him at different places, as will appear in the sequel.

Taking this Ugra-pandiyan for reference, a number of poets and kings could be grouped around him from internal evidence

* The poem quoted at page 2, *note*. *Chilappadhikâram.*

of contemporaneity without having recourse to any legends concerning them. But it is first of all necessary to shew that it is **Probable that Tiruvalluvar was a contemporary of Ugra-Pandiyan.** Apart from the verse in praise of the *Kural* ascribed to him, it is a well-known fact that Tiruvalluvar had a sister by name, or rather title, **Avvaiyar.** This poetess sings of this same Pandiyan and his two friends the Chola Killi, who performed the *Rajasuya*, and the Chêramân Mâvenkô although the names of these personages are not mentioned as such in the poem 367 of the *Purananuru.* But poem 21 of the same collection by Aiyur Mûlangilâr, specifies his victory over Vêngaimârban and the taking of 'the great fortress of the forest Kânappêreyil. It also refers to the fame of this Pandiyan, transcending the skill of poets. This Ugra-Pandiyan is credited with having got the collection *Agananuru* made. Certain mythical achievements are ascribed to one Ugravarma Pandiyan in the *Madura Sthalapurana* and the *Halasya* or *Tiruvilayadal*, which achievements are alluded to in the "Epic of the Anklet."*

Leaving aside Ugra-Pandiyan for a while, the greatest of Avvaiyar's patrons—in fact almost the patrons—were **Adiyaman Neduman Anji** and his son, **Poguttelini.** Their territories were in the modern Mysore province and in the Salem District, with the capital at Tagadur,† identified with Dharmapuri in the latter district, though there was another Tagadur of some consequence in later history in the Mysore District not far from Nanjanagûdu near Mysore town. There was an Adiyaman about the same region who, as the Chola Viceroy was driven across the Kaveri when Talakadu was captured by the famous Ganga Raja, the general of Vishnuvardhana Hoysala before 1117 A. D. Of the many poems the *Purananuru* collection ascribed to Avvaiyar, the great majority

* *Chilappadhikâram*, canto xi., ll. 20—31.

† Mr. Kanakasabhai Pillai identifies this place with Dharmapuri, Salem District. *Vide Ephigraphia Indica*, VI, No. 34, and *ante* XXII, pp. 66 and 143. Mr. F. J. Richards, M.A., I.C.S., informs me that a hill overhanging the town Atûr goes by the name "*Avvaimalai*," the hill of Avvai.

celebrate Anji, one of the last 'seven patrons of letters,' as patronge went in those days. Several of these mention the hero and his son by name. Poem 91 gives the hero's name and refers to the gift to Avvaiyar of the black gooseberry supposed to confer immortality on the lucky eater thereof. The same incident is referred to, with the name of Avvaiyor put in it, in the poem *Criupanuttuppadai** of **Nallur Nattattanar** included in the 'Ten Tamil Idylls' another Sangam collection. The poem has for its special object the celebration of Erumanaddu Nalliyakkôn a petty chief over Vellore, Amur and other places near about, as the most liberal among liberal patrons of those days, *viz.*, the Chera, the Chola and the Pandiya, and the seven last patrons. Poem 99 of the *Purananuru* is of importance, as giving us another clue to a different synchronism of the utmost consequence. This poem celebrates Anji's conquest of Tirukkovilur and states that the hero's fame transcended the capacity of the poets of an older generation, and yet the poet **Paranar** 'sings to-day of the glory of your conquest of Tirukkovilur.'

This mention of **Paranar is of very great importance to literary history.** He was a poet among the Sangam members and is credited with a large number of the *Purananuru* collection. But Paranar's fame should have been greater, had he really enjoyed the patronage of Chenguttuvan Chera, whom he celebrated in the fifth division of another Sangam collection, the 'Ten Tens' (*Padittuppattu.*) The parentage ascribed to Chenguttuvan there agrees word for word almost with that given by the author of the 'Epic of the Anklet, a brother of the king, and is even fuller of particulars. The last verse,† the *Padigam*, written either by a friendly contemporary or disciple or some one else in a similar position, explicitly gives us the names of the hero and the author, and thus leaves us in little doubt as to the correctness of the connection. It is on these two accounts that the commentator of the latter work

* ll. 99—103.

† *Vide* page 10, footnote on page 11, and canto xxix. Pandit Saminatha Iyer's edition recently published, pp. 78—76. *Chilappadhikâram.*

relies for his fuller account of the Chera's history. From the reference to the *Cirupân* made above, it is clear that Avvaiyar enjoyed the patronge of Adiyamân Nedumân Anji. Poem 99 of *Purananuru* refers to Paranar as having celebrated the same patron. The last verse of the fifth division of the 'Ten Tens' connects unmistakably Chenguttuvan with Paranar. Thus then it is clear that **Chenguttuvan Chera, Adiyaman Anji-Avvaiyar and Paranar must have lived**, if not actually at same time, at least **in the same generation.** Chenguttuvan was a remarkably great ruler, and thanks to the efforts of our modern 'Nachchinarkiniyar' Mahamahopadhaya Pandit Saminatha Iyer of the Madras Presidency College, we have two great works composed at his court and in his time, which shed a flood of light on contemporary history and which would go a long way in setling many a knotty point in the literary history of South India. These are the Epic of the Anklet' **(Chilappadhikaram)** and 'the Jewel Belt' **(Manimegalai).** The first is the work of **Ilango,** the younger brother of Chenguttuvan, who, after renouncing civil life, resided at Kunaváyil near Karur (Vanji), the ancient capital of the Chera; and the second, the companion and supplement, though the earlier composed, from the pen of (rather the style of) **Madurai Kula Vanigan Sattan,** otherwise known as Chîtthalaichattanar, "the corn merchant" of Madura. Before proceeding to a consideration of these great works, it is better to dispose of a few other important characters.

Of the last seven patrons celebrated in the *Cirupanattuppadai* of Nallur Nattattanar (believed to be one of the Sangam forty-nine), there is one **Pegan** (otherwise **Vaiyavikkôn Perum Pegan)** who was so liberal (inconsiderately) so as to give a warm covering to a peacock. This same incident is referred to in poem 145 of the *Purananuru* ascribed to Paranar. This personage sometime in his life transferred his affections from his wife Kannahi (to be carefully distinguished from the heroine of the 'epic') and several poets, among whom Paranar, made poetical appeals on her behalf. The others were Kapilar, ·isil Kilar and Perumkuntur Kilar (poems 43—45 both inclusive of the *Purananaru.*) There is considerable similarity of sentiment in these. Poem 343 of the same work is also ascribed to Paranar and it refers to a Kuttuvan very liberal in the donation of wealth 'brought down hill-country and from oversea.'

Passing on to **Kapilar** another Sangam celebrity reputed by tradition* to be the elder brother of Tiruvalluvar, it is found that he had for his patron and friend a chieftain, **Vel Pari**, whose demesne Parambunadu comprised 300 villages and who was master of Parambu **Hill**. Kapilar is credited with having composed the *kurinji* section of the *Aingurunuru*, the seventh of the 'Ten Tens,' the *kurinjippattu* of the 'Ten Idylls' (all Sangam works) and the *Inna* (that which are bad and therefore to be avoided), forty. When Pari fell a victim to the treachery of the three powers, who made a futile attack on him jointly, Kapilar as his chief friend took his two girls with him to be given away in marriage to some person worthy of them and thus do his last duty to his departed friend. Poems 200, 201 and 202 of the *Purananuru* refer to the incident† of Pari's giving a car to the creeper *mullai* and to Kapilar's offering the girls to Vichchikkôn and Pulikadimal ‡ Irungôvêl of Malainadu. Both of them refused to marry girls, and some insult offered as to the social standing of his patron's family the poet resents in poem 202. Poem 201 refers to Irungôvêl having been descended in the forty-ninth generation from the ruler of 'Tuvarai' § who was born from a sacrificial fire. The title Pulikadimal has considerable similarity in its origin to a story which is given as explaining the origin of the Hoysalas in inscriptions of a latter time. The following poem resents Irungovel's refusal to marry the girls and refers to the destruction of Araiyam city, the head-quarters of this family, in consequence of an insult offered

---

* The actual story connecting these is regarded as a fabrication by some scholars.

† *Vide Cirupân.* ‡ He that killed a tiger.

§ 'Tuvarai' may be either Dwaraka in Guzerat or Dwaravati or Dwarasamudra of the Hoysalas.

to the poet Kalathalaiyar * by an ancestor of Irungovel's. The poet further begs, with biting sarcasm, to be pardoned for his having introduced the girls as the daughters of Pari, instead of as the descendants of Evvi a chief in the Pandiya country.

Kapilar himself is connected with the **Chera Mantharam Cheral Irumporal** and spoken of with great regard as a poet by another poet, **Porundhil Ilangiranar.** Poem 126 by **Marokkattu Nappasalaiyar** refers to his having praised **Malaiyaman Tirumudikkari,** who was in possession of Mullur Hill. It incidentally refers to the naval strength of the Chera, likening the futility of the author's attempt at celebrating Kari when Kapilar had done so, to the endeavour to sail a ship in the face of the Chera fleet. Poem 174 by the same author refers incidentally to Mullur Hill, celebrated by Kapilar, and directly to Choliyavenadhi Tirukkannan (otherwise Tirukkilli), who rendered yeoman's service to Peruvirarkilli while in hiding at Mullur. The poem further credits the Malayaman Choliyavenadhi Tirukkannan with having restored the Chola to his position.

Another person that Kapilar celebrates is **Tirumudikkari, ruler of Malainadu,** with his capital at Tirukkovilur and with the hill Mullur. Poems 122 and 123 refer to his having been sought in alliance by the three powers.

Beginning with a consideration of what little is known of these three personages, Avvaiyar, Paranar and Kapilar, we have been introduced to a number of poets and potentates living within a generation of one another. Before proceeding to a consideration of the chief rulers of the age and their geographical location, let us turn aside to glean what we can of contemporary history from the two epics of the age of Chenguttuvan, who was, by far, the most important character of the period and about whom we could gather an amount of information from the above works.

---

* Another poet who celebrates Karikala, and his Chera contemporary, Perumceraladhan. (Poem 65, *Puranânûru.)*

The '**Epic of the Anklet**' is the story of Kovalan (Gopala), and his wife Kannagi, both of the mercantile community of Pugar (Kaverippumbattinam), and has, for its moral, the triumph of the wife's chastity and the vindication of the husband's innocence. The story is as follows in brief outline:—Kovalan, the son of Masattuvan of Pugar was early married to Kannahi, the beautiful daughter of Manaygan of the same place and community; and the marriage was celebrated with great pomp and becoming circumstance, as the two parties were of high social standing. After a while the mother-in-law set her daughter-in-law up independently in a different house in the same city, provided with all that the young couple might need for conducting a successful and virtuous life, as householder and housewife. Sometime after, Kovalan took a fancy for a highly accomplished and exceedingly lovable professional dancing-woman, whose skill in her art was unsurpassed—nay, even unsurpassable. The lover and mistress led a happy life and had a daughter, the only offspring of their affection. Disconsolate as Kannagi was, she never lost her affection for the husband who had thus given her up, and was quite as faithful to him as she would have been under ordinary circumstances. At the conclusion of the annual festival to the god Indra, the usual bathing in the sea brought the festivities to a close. This was a day of enjoyment for all and the whole elegant society of Pugar turned out to the beach to spend the day in music, dancing, and other such amusements. The happy lovers singing to the accompaniment of the '*yâl*' (a Tamil musical instrument now gone out of use) by turns, suspected each the other of having changed his or her affection, from the tenor of the songs. Stung by this imagined bad faith on the part of his sweet-heart Madhavi, Kovalan went home to his house, instead of to hers as usual, and felt quite ashamed of himself for his treatment of the wife, who redoubled her attentions to him since she had seen that something ailed her lord. Overcome with remorse, Kovalan confessed to his wife his position with respect to Mâdhavi and communicated to her his resolution to make amends for his past misconduct by entering on business in Madura on his own account, asking her if she would follow him, should he act upon his resolution. Kannagi signified a ready assent and gave her husband the pair of anklets (*çilambu*), the only thing valuable he had not as yet given away to Madhavi, for providing the requisite capital to the prospective merchant of Madura. That very night the repentant and admiring husband with his faithful spouse started away before dawn unknown to anyone, and took his way along the northern bank of the Kaveri. Picking up the nun Dêvandhî, a few miles above Pugâr, they continued their journey to Srîrangam and Uraiyûr. Thence taking one of the three roads indicated by the Malainâdu Brâhman from Mângâdu (Alaway in Travancore), who was returning from Madura on a pilgrimage to the shrines of Vishnu, they reached the outskirt of the capital city of the Pandiyans. Leaving his tender wife in charge of a hospitable shepherdess and her daughter, he entered Madura city the next day to sell one of the pair of anklets. Not finding a ready sale, as the jewel was of very high value, he wandered long before he was accosted by a goldsmith, who was going palaceward at the head of a number of his apprentices. On Kôvalan's offering the jewel for sale, the wily smith promised to get it sold, with a request that he would keep the jewel with him and wait till he should send for him from the palace whither he was then going. Proceeding gleefully to the royal residence, he reported to the king that the thief who had stolen the queen's anklet had been caught with the jewel in his possession and had been kept waiting under promise of purchase. The king who was much distressed at the loss of the jewel and the pain it caused the Queen, asked that the jewel to be brought 'killing the thief'; he actually meant, asking the man and the jewel to be brought, to kill the man, if guilty. The plot of the goldsmith, the real culprit, succeeded so well that the king was deluded and the innocent hero was murdered, after transacting a pathetic scene much like the one in Shakespear's Richard III. News of this calamity reached Kannag who, in great anger, forgot her usual modesty, and bent upon establishing her husband's innocence and the power of her chastity, walked boldly forth quite, unlike her ordinary self, with the other anklet in her hand and rang the bell of justice in the great gate of the palace. This alarm, quite unheard of in the reign of the then Pandiyan ruler, aroused the suspicions of the hall-porter that something seriously wrong had taken place. The unusual apparition of a young injured woman with an anklet in one of her hands, anger and grief on the countenance, was immediately announced to the king. Admitted without delay into the royal presence, Kannagi proved that the anklet for which her husband suffered death was hers and not the queen's, demonstrating that the jewel in dispute was filled with rubies. The queen affirmed hers was filled with pearls. Kannagi invoked a curse that Madura be consumed by fire for this remissness of her king, who, rather than survive this disgrace he brought upon a line of illustrious rulers, died immediately. The queen followed her consort, and Kannagi left the city by the western gate towards the hill country, where she was to join her husband in a fortnight, as promised by the Goddess of Madura.

This union of the wife and the husband was seen by the hill-tribes, who duly reported the matter to their king, then in camp on the hills with his queen and retinue. At the request of the good queen, the king built a temple and consecrated it to the chaste lady (Pattinî Dêvi) who had undergone so recent an apotheosis.

This is, in the merest outline, the story of the first epic, and the second is a sequel to this. Information of all the proceedings at Madura was given at Pugâr by a Brahman friend of Kôvalan, who, having bathed at Kumari (Cape Comorin, near which was once a river), was baiting at Madura on his homeward journey. The mother and mother-in-law of Kannagi died of grief. The father and father-in-law renounced life and became Buddhistic monks.

Mâdhavî, disconsolate at Kôvalan's sudden disappearance, sent him an importunate appeal to return, while he was yet on his outward journey to Madura. Finding it of no avail, she had been overcome with grief, and when news of Kôvalan's death reached her, she gave up life and all its pleasure to become a lay disciple of a Buddhistic monk; while her daughter just blooming into a woman of rare beauty and womanly grace, entered the Buddhistic cloister. "Jewel-Belt" (Manimêgalai) was her name and her renunciation forms the subject of the epic with her name. The heir-apparent of Pugâr is very deeply in love with her, but she is taken care of by a Goddess, who plays the guardian angel, much like the Ariel of Shakespeare. To save her from the loving prince's ardour, she is removed to an island by the goddess while asleep; and there she is initiated into the Buddhist mysteries. Having understood her past life, she returns to Pugâr with a begging-bowl of extraordinary virtue. The prince still prosecuting his hopeless love, falls a victim to the jealousy of an angel, whose wife's disguise the heroine assumed to keep out her importunate lover, her own husband in a previous life. Consoling the Queen and the King in their sorrow for the loss of their son, she leaves Pugâr (at the mouth of the Kaveri) and proceeds to Vanji (not far from Kranganûr at the mouth of the Periyâr), where she learns all that the teachers of different religious systems have to teach her. Not satisfied with their philosophy of religion, she is directed to Kânchî by her grandfather, who had betaken himself to Vanji in anticipation of Pugâr being overwhelmed by the sea. Manimêgalai proceeds to Kânchî and relieves the place from famine by the use of her begging-bowl. Learning the true philosophy of the Buddha from a saintly monk, she stopped there. This is the merest outline of the two poems, forming a single epic, which are of a dramatic-epic character with something of the narrative in it. Containing, as they do, a great deal of the supernatural, there is yet much that must be regarded as historical. In one word, the setting is poetical, but the back-ground is historical.

The 'Epic of the Anklet' has much to say about the "three great kings of the south" and its companion concerns itself with three likewise; but the place of the Pandiyan is taken by the ruler of Kânchî. To begin with the Chôla kings celebrated by the poets, two names stand out; those of Karikala and Killi, called indifferently Nedumudik-killi, Velvêl killi, Mavan-killi, etc. Of these two, Dr. Hultzsch has the following in his South Indian inscriptions*:—"It will be observed that each of the four documents, which record the names and achievements of these ancient Chôla kings, enumerates them in a different order. One of the four kings, Kôkkilli can hardly be considered a historical person, as he is credited with having entered a subterraneous cave and there to have contracted a marriage with a serpent princess, and as the *Vikkirama Solan Ulâ*, places him before the two mythical kings, Sibi and Kavera."............... Of Karikâla and Kô-chchengan here follows what the same authority has to say: "A comparison of these conflicting statements shews that at the time of the composition of the three documents referred to, no tradition remained regarding the order in which Kô-chchengan and Karikâla succeeded each other. Probably their names were only known from ancient Tamil panegyrics of the same type as *Kalavali* and *Pattinappâlai*. It would be a mistake to treat them as actual ancestors of that Chôla dynasty, whose epigraphical records have come down to us. They must rather be considered as representatives of extinct dynasties of the Chôla country, whose names had survived in Tamil literature either by chance or by specially-marked achievements."

"To Karikala the Leyden grant attributes the building of embankments along the Kaveri river. The same act is alluded to in the *Kalingattupparani* and *Vikkirama Solan Ulâ*. The *Kalingattupparani* adds that he paid 1,600,000 gold pieces to the author of the *Pattinappalai*. According to *Porunarâttuppadai* of Mudathama Kanniyâr the name of the king's father was Ilanjêtchenni. The king himself is there called Karikâl or blackleg or the elephant-leg; while the Sanskritized form of his name Karikala would mean 'death to elephants.'

* Vol. II, Part III, pp. 377 and 378.

He is said to have defeated the Chera and Pandiya kings in battle fought at Vennil. According to the *Chilappadhikâram* his capital was Kaverippûmbattinam. In one of his interesting contributions to the history of ancient Tamil literature, the Hon'ble P. Coomarasami allots Karikâla to the 1st century A. D. This opinion is based on the fact that the commentaries on the *Chilappadhikâram* represent Karikâla as the maternal grandfather of the Chera king, Chenguttuvan, a contemporary of Gajabahu of Ceylon. Mr. Coomarasami identifies the latter with Gajabahu I who, according to the *Mahâvamsa*, reigned from (135 A. D.). With due respect to Mr. Coomarasami's sagacity, I am not prepared to accept this view, unless the identity of the two Gajabahus is not only supported by the mere identity of name but proved by internal reasons, and until the chronology of the early history of Ceylon has been subjected to a critical examination."

A careful examination of the first book of the 'Epic of the Anklet' shows that during the early part of the life of the hero, **the king of Pugar was Karikala Chola.** Apart from the fact that the commentator invariably interprets all references to the ruling king as applying to Karikala (and this in itself is much, as the commentator was one who was thoroughly qualified for the task and can, as such, be expected to embody nothing but correct tradition in his commentaries), there are a number of direct references to him—either by name or by the attribute of his having erected the tiger-emblem on the Himalayas. The last four lines of canto i blesses the ruler "who erected the tiger-emblem on the crest of the Himalayas." There is direct mention of Karikala's name and his rewarding the poet of the *Pâlai* [*Pattinappâlai*]* in one of the manuscripts consulted by the editor; further down, lines 158-160 of canto vi mention as clearly as one could wish Karikala as ruling at the time, and the commentator explains it as such by giving the passage the necessary expansion, not

* Page 44 and 45—Pandit Saminatha Iyer's edition of *Chilapadhikâram*. There is nothing in the lines to lead one to regard them as later interpolations.

to mention the allusive but undoubted reference to the same personage in lines 95-98 of canto v. Of the three Kings praised in canto xvii, there is reference to Karikala's Himalayan exploit in the last stanza in page 400, and this is the last Chola ruler referred to. Canto xxi, lines 11 *et seq.*, clearly state that Karikala's daughter had married the then Chera king, whom she joined when he lost* his life in the sea. These would undoubtedly point to Karikala as having ruled at Kaverippumbattinam till Kovalan's departure for Madura. The supernatural achievements are clearly nothing more than the fanciful way in which these Buddhistic authors attempt to explain even the most ordinary occurrences. The most cursory examination will discover that it is so, and the faith of these authors in the doctrine of *karma* comes in for much that would otherwise be inexplicable in the story.

To return to **Karikala**. He was **the son of Uruvappatter-Ilanjetchenni** and had married among the Nângur Vêl class. He is reputed to have assumed the form of an old judge in order to satisfy the scruples of the parties, who were afraid that, being a youth, he could not bring mature experience to bear upon the question coming up for decision. His name is actually accounted for as having been due to an accident by fire † while yet a baby. He is the hero of the two poems in the "Ten Tamil Idylls," *Porunarattuppadai* of Mudathamakkanniyar and the *Pattinappalai* of Rudirangannanar, for which latter the author received the 16 lakhs of gold pieces mentioned above. He defeated the Chera by name Perum-Cheraladhan and a Pandiyan whose name is not mentioned in the battle of Vennil.‡ This Chera wounded in the back in battle retired to the north in disgrace.§ Rudirangannanar

---

* The text has it that when he was drowned she called out for him. The waves shewed him to her when she joined him and both disappeared, much like Kannagi's union with her husband.

† The 3rd stanza from the *Palamoli* quoted at the end of the *Porunarâttuppadai*.

‡ Lines 143—148. *Porunarâttuppadai.* Vennil is Kovil Venni in the Tanjore District.

§ *Puranânûru* poems 65 and 66.

celebrates another hero, the **Tondaman Ilandirayan of Kanchi** whom tradition traces to the Chola Killi by a "Naga" princess, as stated by Dr. Hultzsch, in the quotation above.

This Killi, otherwise Nedumudi-Killi, is the ill fated **successor of Karikala**, in whose reign a catastrophe befell Pugar and brought the Chola fortunes very low indeed. While luckily there are but a few Karikalas among South Indian rulers, there are a number of Killis,* among whom it is a matter of great difficulty indeed to fasten upon the individual here mentioned. Fortunately for us there are certain distinguishing features which give us the clue. One of the exploits of Chenguttuvan Chera is the victory at Nêrivâyil, a village near Uraiyur (Trichinopoly), where he defeated the nine Killis of the Chola family and thus restored his cousin [brother-in-law] to power. From the 'Epic of the Anklet' and the 'Jewel Belt,' we learn he was the last ruler in Pugar and it was in his reign that the ancient Chola capital was overwhelmed by the sea. It is this Killi, whatever his distinguishing epithet, that is the **father of the Tondaman** referred to by Dr. Hultzsch. While in the *Perum-panattuppadai*, the commentator Nachchinarkiniyar [who must have lived in the 13th century A.D. or thereabouts†] makes the Tondaman the son of a Naga princess with whom the Chola lived in a cave, which is generally taken to mean the nether-world, the 'Jewel-Belt' gives the following much less romantic version of the story, which agrees in all details except the cave, so far as it goes, while accounting for the destruction of Pugar. Without going so far out as the Hades, we find reference to Naga rulers in India and Ceylon, between whom a war once took place for the possession of some Buddha-relic, according to the 'Jewel-Belt.'‡ The same also refers to another race of the Nagas as "naked cannibals." The story goes on to state

* Twelve in *Puranânûru*, and nine in *Chilappadhikaram*.

† Mr. Anavaradha Vinayagam Pillai allots him to the 9th century A.D. (*Christian Coll. Mag.*, XVII), 1900.

‡ We find reference to such wars in *Mahâvamsa*, in the earlier chapters of the work.

that Killi fell in love with a Naga princess, who appeared before him all alone like a damsel from the fairy-land, in what is called the "Kali Kanal"* [the grove by the back-water] at Pugar. After a month of happy life, she left him [and this is explained away by preordination], when she had taken her residence in an island near the coast† 300 miles away from Pugar. Sometime after she became the mother of a beautiful son, she sent the child to the father through a merchant, whose ship called at the island on its homeward journey. While nearing Pugar, the ship got wrecked off the coast and the baby's fate was not known for certain. On hearing of this disaster, the king ordered a thorough search to be made and in his paternal anxiety forgot his duty to the God Indra, whose annual festival had been forgotten. The wrath of the God shewed itself, very likely, in a storm-wave which destroyed Pugar completely.‡

This account taken from the 'Jewel-Belt' of the birth of the Tondaman makes Dr. Hultzsch's objection as to the myth, lose edge, and therefore it is quite possible—nay, even historical—that there was a human ruler by name Killi, who ruled at Pugar after Karikala.

[*Note.*—The descent into the Hades, therefore, will have to be regarded as an eastern figure of speech and nothing more. There are other incidents throughout these epics, which interpreted literally would be quite as absurd; and these are easily accounted for by the author's belief in the doctrines of Karma and re-births, the main pillars of the Buddhistic faith, as also to a modified extent of the Brahmanic. It is this that makes them attempt to account for actual

* This Kali-Kanal is refered to in canto vii as the place of resort of pleasure-seekers—nay, a veritable "lover's arbour" in Pugar.

† *Vide Manimêgalai* note, pp. 97 and 98. The island of Ceylon, in which is Adam's Peak, is sacred to the Buddhists. This hill is now known as Samantakudam and Samanelai, but referred to in the works as Samantam and Samanoli.

‡ There is a story of similar import with respect to a Ceylonese king, whose wife was abducted by a Chola king under similar circumstances. There are no grounds to connect the two at prnt, at any rate.ese

phenomena by causes supernatural. This modern European critics fail to bear in mind, and hence all appears grotesquely legendary and absurdly fabulous. These remarks find their full application in the 'Jewel-Belt', though there is hardly any Indian work of a quasi-religious or ethical character in criticising which one could afford to forget them.]

The destruction of Pugar referred to above accounts for the association of Killi with Uraiyur at the end of the 'Epic of the Anklet,' in the course of which the catastrophe to Pugar must have happened. The ruler at Kanchi during the period, according to the 'Jewel-Belt,' was an **Ilam Killi, the brother of Kalaar Killi.**

This last ruler of Pugar is referred to in the 'Jewel-Belt' with the following adjuncts indifferently, *viz.*, Vadivêl-killi, Velvêl-killi, Mavan-killi and Nedumudi-killi. With the help of his younger brother **Ilango** [perhaps Ilamkilli of Kânchi], who was probably the heir-apparent as the term would indicate, he defeated the Cheras and the Pandiyas on the banks of the river Kâri.* The three poems concerning this personage in the *Purananuru* refer to his having been besieged at Uraiyur and Amur by Nalam-killi. After the destruction of Pugar he must have been reduced to the woeful plight from which Chenguttuvan Chera must have relieved him by his victory at Nêrivâyil † over the nine Chola princes who forgot their allegiance to the Killi. This is borne out by the enmity between Nedumudi-killi and Nalamkilli indicated in poems 44, 45 and 47 of *Puranânûru*. There are besides a number more of Killis, each with a distinguishing epithet which would support the existence of the nine Killis [Killi being a generic name of the Cholas like Senni, etc.]. The author of these poems, **Kovil Kilar**, celebrates another Killi who died at Kulamuttam. None of these Killis is associated with

* Pandit Saminatha Iyer's edition of *Manimêgalai*, page 174, canto xix. lines 124-130.

† Nerivayil in later history belonged to the Kshatriya Sikhamani Valanadu, *i.e.*, the region round Uraiyur, and the royal secretary of Virarajendra was the owner of this village as also of Tali Tirappanangadu. *South Indian Inscriptions*, Vol. III.

Pugar. In fact neither in the *Puranânûru* nor in the *Sirupân âttuppadai* do we find the city of Pugar associated with these Cholas.

Leaving aside the Cholas, we find the whole time, during which the incidents narrated in the two epics, took place, taken up by **Chenguttuvan Chera**, whose capital was at Vanji [Karur] at the mouth of the Periyar on the west coast. His exploits are recorded in some detail in these works and the others referred to already. His father and uncle are celebrated in the two preceeding sections of the "Ten Tens." His chief achievements were a naval victory over the 'Kadambu,' two invasions of the north with victories on the banks of the Ganges over Kanaka and Vijaya, sons of Balakumara and the victories at Nerivayil and Viyalur [there is a Viyalur connected with Nannan, an ancestor of Vichchikkon, whom Kapilar celebrates in poem 200 of the *Puranânûru*]. Like his father, Chenguttuvan also claims to have cut out the bow-emblem on the Himalayas.

Coming to the Pandiyas of Madura, we have two names in the 'Epic of the Anklet', *viz.*, **Nedum Cheliyan**, victor over the "Aryan army," and **Ilam Cheliyan**, who was Viceroy at Korkai when Nedum Cheliyan died at Madura. Before discussing these names we have to dispose of one other Pandiyan of importance in literary history. When Tiruvalluvar submitted the *Kural* to the Sangam critics, the king was **Ugra-Pandiyan**, victor over the "big forest fort [Kanappereyil] under the chief Vengaimarban." The *Tiruvilaiyâdal Purânam* ascribes to him some achievements which are of a legendary character, though some might have been possible. These are the very achievements* ascribed to a Pandiya ruler by the Malainadu [hill-country] Brahman from Mangâdu, **(Alangadu or Alavayi)** then at Uraiyur in the course of a pilgrimage to the shrines of Vishnu, who directed Kovalan to Madura from Uraiyur. This praise would lose all point unless it referred to the ruling Pandiyan when the Brahmin pilgrim

* Canto xi, lines 23-31. There are besides references to his achievements in connection with the ruling Pandiyan in many places throughout the work.

sojourned at Madura, on his visit to Tirumal-irunjôlai. The author of the epic clearly designates him the Pandiyan Nedum Cheliyan "victor over the Aryan forces," whatever these forces might have been. There are a number of references throughout the work to the erecting of the fish-emblem on the Himalayas. It is the boast of Karikala Chola and Ugra-Pandiyan, Nedumçêralâdhan [father of Chenguttuvan], that they cut out their respective emblems on the Himalayas. These achievements are clearly ascribed to the reigning Pandiyan in the commencing and the concluding lines of canto xvii. Thus then the Ugra-Pandiyan* of the *purânas* and tradition could not have been any other than the ill-starred Pândiyan Nedum Cheliyan of the 'Epic of the Anklet.' Avvaiyar's reference to Paranar referred to above would agree quite well with this identification, as in accordance with that reference, Paranar should have been the earlier of the two.

The successor of the Pandiyan, apparently his son, **Pandiyan Ilam Cheliyan**, otherwise Vettivêl-Cheliyan, was in Korkai when his father died and succeeded to his father's estate in the course of the story. We are vouchsafed no other information, except that he propitiated the names of the injured lady, Kannagi, by the sacrifice of 100 goldsmiths [perhaps a massacre of that class of artisans]. Probably his reign was short and uneventful. He must have been succeeded by Pandiyan Nedum Cheliyan, victor at Talayalanganam † over the two other kings and seven chiefs. Kapilar is connected with prince **Mantharam Cheral Irumporai** of the "elephant-look" by **Porundhil Ilam Kiranar** in poem 53 of *Puranânûru*. This Chera was ruling over Tondi [Quilandy, and not the Cholan Tondi, on the east coast now in the Ramnad *zamîndârî*].

---

* Stanza 4, bottom of page 490. Mr. Kanakasabhai Pillai in his interesting papers on "The Tamils 1800 Years Ago," makes Ugra Pandiyan the contemporary of the successor of the Killi, the grandson of Karikala. This would bring Tiruvalluvar's *Kural* too late for quotation by the friendly authors of the two epics, as the *Kural* received the Sangam approval under Ugra-Pandiyan. [*Madras Review*, Vol. II, No. 6].

† He must have been particularly young when he came to the throne, *Puram*, 7.

and was the master of Kolli Malai* [a hill in the Salem District quite on the border of Trichinopoly]. His position in this region would have been possible only in the light of Chenguttuvan's victories over the Kongus at Chengalam [red-field], at Viyalur, about the same region, and over the nine Cholas at Nêrivâyil [near Trichinopoly]. This personage was taken prisoner by the Pandiyan Nedum Cheliyan † of Talayalanganam fame. At this latter place, the young Pandiyan overthrew the "Tamil army" under the two kings and 'seven chiefs.' This Pandiyan was a great celebrity in literature and in his reign flourished a number of poets of the Sangam fame. He is the hero of Mangudi Marudhanar's *Maduraikkânji* and Narkirar's *Nedunalvâdai* among the "Ten Tamil Idylls." He was himself, like several other rulers of those days, including his grandfather, a poet. There are a number of poems relating to him in the *Puranânûru* collection. Thus we see that during the course of the story, the **rulers of Pugar** were Karikala and his grandson Ko killi; ‡ of Madura, Nedum Cheliyan identified with Ugra Pandiyan and Ilam Cheliyan followed later by Nedum Cheliyan, victor over the Tamil army at Talayalanganam; The Chera ruler all the time at Karur [Vanji] was Chenguttuvan Chera, the brother of the author of the epic and the patron of the author of the 'Jewel-belt,' the father and the uncle of this personage having been the heroes of 2nd and 3rd section of the "Ten Tens." Chêy, (prince) of the "elephant-look" must have been his son and viceroy of the newly-conquered territories.

These were the sovereigns of the three kingdoms who flourished in the generation of the literary celebrities headed by the names chosen at the commencement, *viz.*, **Avvaiyar,**

* The last lines of canto xiv, the 'Epic of the Anklet,' refer to the reigning Chera as the ruler over the country between the Himalayas with the bow-emblem and Kolli Malai.

† "Epic of the Anklet," canto xxviii, lines 115-125. Cheliyan is again a generic name like Pandiyan, and the father or the son have the adjunct "big" or "young," much as 'Smith, senior or junior.'

‡ Mr. Kanakasabhai Pillai places a Nalamkilli between these two. [*Madras Review*, Vol. II, No. 7.]

Paranar and Kapilar. These were the three stars of the first magnitude in the literary firmament, as those in the political, of South India. Other poets there were and patrons likewise. Of the latter, mention has already been made of Pari of Parambunadu and Parambu hill; Kari of Tirukkôvilur in Malainadu and Mullur Hill; Irungovel of Araiyam in the Western hill-country of the "Tuvarai * family with the special distinction of having killed a tiger to save a saint absorbed in contemplation;" Pegan of Nallur in Malainadu [hill-country]; And Adiyaman Anji of Tagadur and the horse-hill, overthrown according to the 8th section of the "Ten Tens" by the Perum Chêral who overthrew Tagadur. These are all mentioned by name as well as by distinguishing achievements, most of them in a somewhat fabulous garb in the *Sirupanâttuppadai* of Nallur Nattattanar. Besides these, we have already mentioned the prince Chera of the "elephant look," ruler of Tondi and master of Kolli Hill. To come to the poets, in addition, to the three already referred to, we must mention here only a few of the more important, such as **Tiruvalluvar, Ilangovadigal, Siththalai Sattanar, Rudirangannanar, Mudathamakkanniyar, Mangudi Marudhanar, Nakkirar** and others, whose works are held even to-day in high esteem by the Tamil world as masterpieces in their respective departments. Some of the rulers were themselves poets of some merit, and Avvaiyar was not the only poetess. The two young daughters of Pari could compose verses and the elegiacs ascribed to them is proof of their ability in this direction. There is besides a poem in *Purananuru* ascribed to the wife of Bhuta Pandiyan, who performed *satti* on the funeral pyre of her husband.† These names raise a strong presumption in favour

* Tuvarai might have been either Dvaraka in Guzerat or Dvaravati or Halibad in Mysore; but the latter does not appear till much later, and the name Tuvarai in classical works is always taken to mean Dvaraka.

† [Besides the three poetesses mentioned, there are Adhimanthiyar, Vellividiyar, Kakkaipadiniyar, Nappasaliyar, Masathiyar and others enumerated more than thirty in number whose poems are found in the "Eight Collections" of the last Sangam. It will be interesting to our readers to learn that, of the poetesses above mentioned, Adhimanthiyar was the daughter of the Chola Kari-kala I. and the mother of the celebrated Chenguttuvan, and who lost her *lovely* husband in the sea and perished with him in the rolling waves. And it is also known that as poetess she is senior to the well-known Avvaiyar. Ed.]

of the view that, as the age of Chenguttuvan [including in it a generation either way] was one of great literary activity, it might have been the time when the Sangam activity was at its height.* This was the age when the creed of the Buddha was in the ascendant, which, like all other reform movements of a later time, gave a powerful impetus to the development of the vernaculars of the country. Although the Sangam is not mentioned as such in these early works, we find the **cultivation of Tamil specially associated with Madura**, which is often referred to as "Tamil Kudal,"† despite the fact that a large number of poets mentioned above flourished in other Courts. In the traditional lists of Sangam celebrities we find mention of the names of most of the authors referred to above. It is not improbable, therefore, **that a board of censors like the Sangam** existed about this age at Madura.

Without pausing to examine what other literary men could be grouped along with those spoken of already, we might pass on to the consideration of the more important question of the **probable age of this great literary activity in South India.** The two chief epics—the 'Epic of the Anklet. and the 'Jewel-Belt.'—were Buddhistic, the latter more so than the former; and the other works of the age show considerable Buddhistic influence and follow in this order with regard to dates of composition. The *Kural* is the earliest of the major works, as there are quotations from this work in the companion epics, which even acknowledge the quotations. The two epics must have been composed about the same period—the 'Jewel-Belt' preceding 'the Epic ofthe Anklet; ' *Aganânûru* miscellany is ascribed to Ugra Pandiyan, before whom the

* It will be clear from the above that the author of the *Kural* could not have been much earlier than the friendly authors of the epics. Still they quote with great respect from the *Kural*. This could only be if the *Kural* were authoritatively approved of after being read out before the Sangam, Siththalai Sattan being one of the august body. Ilango, however, was not among this body, although he quotes from the *Kural* likewise.

† *Sirupan* and *Purananuru* and *Kalingattupparaṇi*, of a later age. [Manikkavacagar of the 4th cent. A. D. also alludes to the Sangam in his *Kôvaiyar*, as "கூடலின் ஆய்ந்த ஒண்டமிழ்" Ed.]

Kural received the Sangam imprimatur. The *Kundalakèsi* is another Buddhistic work and, so far as we know it at present, of a controversial character, much like the 'Jewel-Belt' in plan of work. This was followed by the *Nilakèsittirattu* which attempts a refutation of the *Kundalakesi* and must, therefore, be of a later age. If this general course of literary activity is correctly indicated by the editor of 'Sen Tamil,' whose account is relied on here, and if we can fix the probable period of **this literary activity**, this will prove **the sheet anchor in the literary chronology of South India.**

In the midst of the confused tangle of mere names and names of similar sound and meaning, we have, luckily, just a few distinct characters and characteristics that make the attempt not altogether hopeless, provided the question be approached in the spirit of unbiassed enquiry. Athough **Killi** is quite a common name among the Chola rulers, **Karikala** is somewhat uncommon. Chenguttuvan is definite enough and his Ceylon contemporary Gajabahu's name occurs, luckily for students of Tamil history, but twice among 174 names unlike Vikramabahu, for instance. *The Kalingattupparani*, a work composed between [1111—1135 A. D.] refers to Karikala and Ko-killi in the reverse order, Killi being followed by Kochengan, Karikala following both. There appears, from the *Purananuru*, to have been a Killi in the third generation before Karikala; but the Chola succession is fixed as follows with respect to this, taking only such names as are specifically mentioned in the order given below:—Ilanjetchenni, his son Karikala, his Grandson Nedumudi-Killi. The *Kalingattupparani*, like the great commentator who must have lived after Jayam Kondan, the author of this work, ascribes to Killi the descent into the Hades. It is just possible that there was a mistake made, as to the particular Killi whose union with the Naga princess was thus described by later writers. If this were so, the Karikala of the Himalayan fame could not have been Kullottunga I. (1070—1118 A. D.) certainly, nor the Viceroy of Kôli [Uraiyur] in the reign of his father-in-law, Rajendra [1053—1060 A. D.]. There is one other Karikala of the later dynasty* whose epigraphical records are available to us—Aditya Karikala [*circa* 950—985 A. D.] who killed Vira Pandiyan in battle, as if in sport. But the author of the *Kalingattupparani* places Karikala three names before Viranarayana or Parantaka I. while Aditya was the eldest son of Parantaka, a grandson of the first of that name. So then we are driven to the necessity of looking for **this Karikala far earlier than 900 A. D.**

It was shewn above that the works themselves point to an age when the religion of the Buddha was in the ascendant as the probable period when the works under consideration —at least the greatest of them—were composed. Buddhism was overthrowm by about the 7th century A. D. when Hiuen Thsang was travelling through India, and when Tirujnanasambanda flourished. About 862 A. D., a battle was fought between Varaguna Pandiyan † and the western Ganga king Sivamara, at Sri Parambi [Tirupparambiyam near Kumbhakonam]. This would not have been possible had the Cholas been at all powerful. Nor do the works of the age under review mention the Gangas as powerful. We are at this period (750—850 A. D.) passing out of the Pallava ascendency in South India which must have begun about 500 A. D., if not earlier, with Vishnugopa of Kanchi, the contemporary of Samudragupta. There is no reference in the works under notice to such premier position of the Pallavas or even the Tondaman *rajas*—the only Tondaman of the period figuring as a minor chief, Kanchi being a Chola viceroyalty. In the Rayakotta ‡ plates, a Pallava king by name Skandasishya, who must have been earlier than Vishnugopa claims descent from Asvattaman through a Naga princess. Perhaps by this time the origin of Ilandirayan had been so far forgotten as to

---

* For a list of this dynasty of kings, see the table prefixed to my article, "The Chola Ascendency in South India" *(Madras Review)* for November 1902, or the *South Indian Inscription*, Vol. III, Part II, recently published.

† *Annual Report for Epigraphy*, 1905-06, Part II, p. 25, and *Epigraphia Indica*, Vol. VIII, p. 295 and 319.

‡ No. 8 : *Epigraphia Indica*, Vol. V.

make this credible. These considerations lead us to an earlier period for Karikala. This personage is associated with Pugar even in tradition, and the 'Jewel-Belt' tells us in unmistakable language **that Pugar was submerged in Killi's reign.** All the poems in the *Purananuru* about Killi, a number of them with distinguishing epithets, connect them with Uraiyur, and none of them is connected with Pugar. Uraiyur figures as a considerable town in the 'Epic of the Anklet.' Even the *Sirupanarruppadai* does not mention Pugar. This is a very important circumstance as will appear presently.

When **Chenguttuvan** performed an elaborate sacrifice on the occasion of **the consecration of the temple to Pattini Devi** [the heroine of the 'Anklet'], **there was present**, among others **Gajabahu of Lanka** surrounded by sea [as opposed to Mavilangai of Erumanattu Nalliyakkon]. This Gajabahu of Ceylon, Ilam Cheliyan of Madura, and Killi of Uraiyur, built temples to the same deity, following the lead of the Chera. The question now is whether this Gajabahu is the first or the second of the name. The first Gajabahu ruled as monarch of all Ceylon from 113-135 A. D.; the second as one of three from 1142—1164 A.D. as in the list appended to Miss. Duff's *Chronology of India.* Dr. Hultzsch's challenge to the Honourable Mr. Coomarasamy is to establish by internal evidence that the Gajabahu mentioned was the first and not the second of the name. As to the other part of his objection, it must have become clear from the above that for the myth about Killi, later writers alone are responsible; and enough direct evidence has been adduced to show that Karikala was ruling at Pugar when Kovalan began life as a married man, and that his daughter was the wife of the Chera king then reigning. To return to Gajabahu; let us for the sake of argument take him to be the second of the name. We know something of the history of South India in the middle of the 12th century and the geographical distribution of powers. The Chola rulers ought to have been either Vikrama or Kulottunga; the rulers of Madura, either Vira Pandiyan or Vikrama Pandiyan, the sovereigns of the Chera country were Vira Kerala Varman and Vira Ravi Varman; of the Mysore country, Vishnuvardhana and his son, Narasimha. There were no separate rulers at Kanchi, except in the sense that it was an alternative capital of the Cholas. There was an Adiyaman, no doubt, about this period [somewhat earlier], but he was the Chola Viceroy at Talakad [not connected with Tagadur], who was driven across the Kaveri by Ganga Raja, the famous general of Vishnuvardhana. There were no Kongu rulers such as are mentioned in the 'Epic of the Anklet.' Gajabahu himself was in no plight to come to Vanji * [Karur] at the mouth of the Pêrâr, not far from the modern Kranganur [Kodungalur]. Gajabahu was fighting his own battles nearer home with his two neighbours Mânâbharana and Parakramabahu, and it was all he could do to keep himself from being permanently overwhelmed.

The first Gajabahu invaded the Chola country to bring back the inhabitants of Ceylon, carried off by the Chola army on a previous invasion of the island during his father's reign they were then in bondage at 'the city of Kaveri in the country of Soli.' He brought back besides the relics and the begging-bowl of the Buddha ["which aforetime had been carried away by the Dhamilas"]. The *Rajaratnakari* while ascribing the same achievements to him, states that the Ceylonese went of their own accord "to serve at the river Kaveri." † He is there said to have brought a number of the Tamils and settled them in Ceylon. In the *Rajavali*, however, there is an even more elaborate version. The ruler is there called Rajabahu [which may be due to a mislection]. He was accustomed to make solitary night-rounds; when he heard the wailings of a widow in her house, for her two sons had been taken captive by the king of 'Soli Ratta.' The *adigars* [officers] failing to discover anything wrong, the king

* Vanji itself was not the capital of the Chera at the time. The capital of Kerala was then Quilon, and during the period of the Chola ascendncy (900—1300 A. D.)

† Vol. II, pages 57-58. This mention of the river instead of the town would shew that when the *Rajaratnakari* was compiled the existence of the town was passing into oblivion.

sent for the woman and learnt from her that 12,000 families had been carried away, "when the king of Soli Ratta made his descent upon the island." The same achievements as in the previous account are recorded, with the addition "that the king of Ceylon also, upon that occasion, brought away the foot ornaments of Pattini Devi * and also the four arms of the gods." This Pattini Devi could have been no other than the heroine of the epic, who was known as Pattini Devi or Pattini Kadavul. This must have been regarded as a valuable relic in those days, when relics played such a prominent part in religion. As to the begging-bowl of the Buddha, a bowl of extraordinary virtue had been brought by Manimegalai from an island south of Pugar, where there was a Buddha seat as well, which had the divine quality of letting people into the secrets of their former existence, a belief in which was one of the cardinal doctrines of Buddhism. The 'Jewel-Belt' also states that two Naga kings fought for the possession of this Buddha-seat. These then are the native accounts of the Ceylonese chronicles with respect to Gajabahu I.; but, unfortunately, the reference to Pattini Devi does not occur in the earlier compilations. This is matter for great regret. It must, however, be noticed that all these works were compiled from earlier writings and living tradition. Here follows what the learned translator of the works has to say about them:—"So carefully has the text been handed down that the discrepancies found to exist between the more ancient and modern copies are very slight indeed. The *Rajavali* is a work of different hands and compiled from local histories; it is used as a corollary or addition to the two preceding works, continuing the narrative through the struggles between the Portuguese and their rivals, the Dutch, etc."

All tradition, therefore, and the historical circumstances attending the stories of these epics point to the **first Gajabahu,**

* The distinction between the Chola country and other parts of South India is not carefully made in the *Mahâvamsa*. Sometimes they specially talk of Soli Ratta at others of Malabar generally, meaning not the Malabar Coast necessarily, but India generally.

as the Ceylon ruler who was present at the celebration of the sacrifice by Chenguttuvan chera and if the *Rajavali* could be relied on, the conclusion would be forced upon us. As it is, however, there is but little ground to connect these events with the second Gajabahu, as some scholars would have it.

As to the date of the first Gajabahu, the chronicle gives 113—135 A. D. as the period of his reign. Whatever be the real worth of this actual date, we have little reason to regard that of his successor namesake as inaccurate. It has been pointed out that the middle of the 12th century could not possibly be the time when the poets flourished. There is the *Kalingattupparani*, the date of composition of which could not have been much later than 1111 A. D., certainly not later than 1118 A. D. Sundaramurti Nayanar, whom the late Mr. Sundaram Pillai placed in the 8th century A. D. refers to Pari * the patron of Kapilar, and the general tenor of the Epic points to Buddhistic times, which the 12th century was not. Taking the Buddha Nirvana, at 487 B. C. instead of 543 B. C., as recognised by most authorities now, the reign of Gajabahu I. go up to 169—191 A. D. Until it is proved that the earlier dates of the *Mahavamsa* are unreliable † [except for this error], these dates will have to stand, and the **period of the greatest Literary activity in Tamil must thus be put down as the 2nd and 3rd centuries of the Christian era at the latest.** This will be quite consistent with the power of the Tamils in the centuries preceding the Christian era, when they several times invaded Ceylon and imposed themselves on the Ceylonese as usurpers, about the middle of the 1st century B. C. These facts coupled with the emperor Asoka's reference to these Tamil powers, along with the five

---

* The reference is to the complaint which the devotee makes in respect to the lack of liberality in people in his days, although one should choose to describe a miser as a patron liberal as 'Pari,' much as Bacon complains of learned men turning Faustina into Lucretia.

† Prof. Rhys Davids finds the chronicle borne out in important details by the inscriptions among the finds of the Sanchi Tope, etc. (*Buddhist India* pp. 299-300); page 1 *et seq.*, *J. R. A. S.* 1908; *Indian Review*, May, 1908; the *Date of the Buddha* by Mr. Gopala Iyer.

Hellenistic potentates, warrants great probability with respect to the high state of civilisation of the Tamils.

Besides the mention of Gajabahu, we find mention of a number of other rulers in the course of the 'Epic of the Anklet,' who were some of them friendly and others hostile. The friendly kings were the "hundred *karnas*," who provided Chenguttuvan with a fleet of ships with which to cross the Ganges, when he invaded the Northern country to punish Kanaka and Vijaya, sons of Bâlakumâra, who spoke disparagingly of the Tamil rulers. These brothers were helped by Uttara, Vichitra, Rudra, Bhairava, Chitra, Singa, Dhunuthara and Sveta.* Mr. Kanakasabhai takes the "hundred *karnas*" as equal to Sâtakarnin of the *Matsyapurâna*. But against this, there is the objection that the Tamil poet mentions 'the hundred persons, the *karnas*;'† and in one place the author even speaks of "the *karnas*" without the hundred.‡ Besides, as would appear from Dr. Bhandarkar's *Dekhan*, the name Satakarnin was that of a dynasty and not of only one ruler. The name Satakarnin alone appears in the early part of the list and the date is 40 B.C. to 16 A.D. [see 166, *Bombay Gazetteer*, Vol. I., Part II.] The word itself could be taken to mean "keen eared" (rather than hundred-eared), figuratively. It is hard to understand how a contemporary could have rendered it with the number attached not to the ears but to men. Besides, these were ruling in Southern India, although Magadha was included in their dominions. So then, even if the "hundred *karnas*" meant Satakarnin, the particular sovereign might have been Yajna Sri who ruled from 154—174 A. D. in the Maharashtra, and 172—202 A. D. in Telingana. If this be so, we have also a Vijaya, mentioned in all the *Puranas*, who was in Telingana from 202—208 A. D., but as against this, there is the objection that Chenguttuvan crossed Ganges and fought with Vijaya and his brother on the northern bank of Ganges. This notwithstanding, that Chenguttuvan must have flourished about this time, could be inferred from

* Chilap. canto. xxvi. ll. 180-185. † Chilap. canto. xxvi. l. 149.

‡ Chilap. canto. xxvi. p. 177.

the fact that Chenguttuvan's father, Pandiyan Nedumcheliyan and Karikala all claim victory over the Aryan forces. It is very likely that the Tamil forces helped in the overthrow of the foreigners by Gôtamiputra Sâtakarnin and the direct mention of gifts to Karikala by the Rajas of Bundelkhand [Vajranâdu], Magadha and Malava [Avanti] could not be altogether a figment of the imagination, since it is so very definite. **All circumstances attending point to the 2nd century A. D. as the era of Chenguttuvan;** and the era of the greatest literary activity may be taken to be the 2nd and 3rd centuries after Christ.

Buddhism was introduced into South India during the last quarter of the 3rd century B. C. It must have taken some time to strike root, and in those days must have been somewhat slow in spreading. Judging from the exposition of it, as shown in the "Jewel Belt," we might take it that it was as yet so free from any element of corruption as to evoke the admiration of even Christian scholars, like the learned translator of the Ceylonese chornicles. The early centuries after Christ may, therefore, be regarded as the age of Buddhistic ascendency in South India. When Fa Hian was travelling in India, there was already the early signs of revulsion, and Brahmanism returned to the fray. In the next two or three centuries Buddhism was swept off the country and the restoration of Brahmanism was completed when Hiuen Thsang came to India, chiefly through the agency in the Tamil country of the earlier Caiva devotees and some among the Vaishnava. From this time the struggle is not so much between Buddhism and Brahmanism, as between the latter and Jainism.

In the first century of the Christian era then, we find India south of the Tungabhadra thus politically divided. If we start at the source of the Kaveri and follow its course till it meets the Amaravati near Karur, and then go up the latter river continuing our journey till we reach the Palnis and the Western Ghauts, we shall have marked the land-boundary of the Chera sphere of influence. If we take a straight south-easterly line from Karur till we reach the sea, east of Zamindari of Sivaganga and south of the old Chola town of

Tondi, the south of this line would be the Pandiya, and north of it the Chola sphere of influence. It must not be understood that the territory alloted to each power was always directly under it. The frontier regions were always of doubtful allegiance, as could be seen from the care with which rulers in those days fortified and strenthened frontier towns. So far as the Cholas were concerned, they had always prominently before them the strategical advantages of Uraiyur on the west and Kanchi on the north, although their cheif city was Pugar on the sea-coast. Karur was the meeting place of the three powers and it was in its neighbourhood that many a hard-fought battle took place. This central region, particularly the hilly portion, was therefore filled with petty chieftancies owing allegiance, so long as it could be enforced, to one or other of these powers, constituting a group of frontier "buffer states." Thus there was Irungôvêl north of the Mysore District and on the frontiers of Coorg. Next to him was the Adiyaman in the southern-half of the Mysore District and part of the Salem with his headquarters at Tagadur. He belonged to the Chera family. South of this must have been the territory of Pegan with Nallur for his headquarters, the country round the Palnis; between the two last was probably Parambunadu of Pari. Next follows the Kongu country, which we might put down as including a part of the Coimbatore and Salem Districts. In a line east of this is the hill-country of Kâri with its headquarters, Tirukkovilur. South of this is the Chola country proper, and north the province or kingdom, according to circumstances, of Kanchi, South of the Palghat gap and in the Pandiya country was the chieftancy of A'ay round Podiyil Hill in the Western Ghats. On the opposite side round Korkai were the territories of Evvi. During the latter part of the reign of Chenguttuvan there was a Chera probably a Viceroy only, holding a tract of country extending from the Kolli Malais* to Tondi on the coast, with the Chola and the Pandiya countries on either side. This was the prince Chera of "elephant-look" [probably he had small deep-set eyes]. The above appears to have been the geographical

* This was the tract taken from O'ri by his enemy Kari and given to the Chera.

division of the country. This kaleidascopic arrangement vanished and another pattern presented itself with every turn that affairs took.

If we call the age under consideration the age of the Chera ascendency, as Chenguttuvan Chera appears to have been at one time in his life the arbiter of the destinies of this part of the country, we pass on gradually from this into a struggle, the Chera supremacy being shaken by the Pandiyan. Here we lose the thread till we come to about A. D. 400, when the Pallavas rise into importance. The Pallava ascendency begins with Vishnu-gopa of Kanchi, the contemporary of Samudragupta, and reaches its grand climacteric under Narasimhavarman, the destroyer of Badmi [Vatapi] the Chalukya capital about 640 A. D. A century hence we find the Gangas and Pandiyas fighting near Kumbakonam. This *role* the Pandiyas play several times in history. Their position at the farthest end of the peninsula gives them safety. It is only when the frontier powers fall, that we see the Pandiyas asserting themselves. Throughout history the South Indian powers had to oppose the incursion of the Dekhan powers, and from the rise of the Pallavas we can have a clear idea of the general position of the South Indian powers. Varaguna Pandiyan succeeded in chasing the Gangas back into their territory. In another century a new dynasty of the Cholas rise into eminence and achieve an ascendency, matched only by that of the latter empire of Vijayanagar in its best days. The decline of the Cholas again brings into prominence the Pandiya in the south and the Hoysalas in the north. Both alike of these powers are overwhelmed in that great wave of Moslem invasion under Malik Kafur. The Muhammadan is beaten back by the heroic efforts of a number of chiefs and this movement culminates in the establishment of the Vijayanagar empire in the middle of the 14th century. The fall of this empire brings the history of Hindu rule in South India practically to a close, and the Maratha Empire belongs to a different chapter of Indian history.

S. KRISHNASWAMY AIYENGAR, M. A.

THE

Ten Tamil Idyls: I.

BY

The Late Prof. P. SUNDARAM PILLAI, M.A.

AMONG the ancient Tamil classics, if we exclude works that are more or less distinctly grammatical or ethical the 'Ten Idyls' and the 'Five Epics' deserve the most prominent mention. The Idyls are, as the name implies, richly wrought descriptive poems in the most finished style. They are charming portraits of Nature in some of her pleasant and striking moods, and for soberness of thought and accuracy of representation they will bear comparison with anything in the whole realm of literature. In them critics will seek in vain for that idle accumulation of hyperbolical conceits which characterizes the Tamil poems of more modern times. It is to be hoped that as these immortal works of antiquity become better known and appreciated, that childish delight in riotous imagination which now passes for poetic taste will give way to a more soberminded and judicious estimate of the true functions of poesy.

The Idyls as approved and compiled by the ancient Madura College are ten in number, and they are as follows:—

1. *Thiru Murugâttuppadai*, by Nakkîrar, dedicated to Muruga, the war god.

2. *Porunarâttuppadai*, by Mudattama Kanniâr, dedicated to Karikâla Chôla.

3. *Pânarâttuppadai* (Minor), by Nattattanar, dedicated to Nalliyakôdan.

A reprint from the Christian College Magazine, Vol. VIII, March, 1891.

4. *Pânarâttuppadai* (Major), by Uruttiram Kannanâr, dedicated to Ilamtirayan.

5. *Mullaippâddu*, by Napputanar.*

6. *Madurai Kânji*, by Mamkudi Marutanar, dedicated to Nedum Cheliyan.

7. *Nedunal Vâdai*, by Nakkîrar, dedicated to Nedum Cheliyan.

8. *Kurinchippâddu*, by Kapilar, dedicated to Pirakattan, an Aryan king.

9. *Paddina Pâlai*, by Uruttiram Kannanâr, dedicated to Karikala Chôla.

10. *Malaipadukadâm*, by Perum Kausiganar, dedicated to Nannan.

These are the names of the Ten Idyls, their authors, and the persons in whose honour they were composed; and they will probably all alike sound strange to modern ears. But the Tamil student will recognize among the authors named a few of the most celebrated poets of the Madura College. Of the eight authors mentioned, five are among those who are said to have conducted the famous sessions of that College when the immortal *Kural* was approved and accepted. These five are:—Nakkîrar, Nattattanar, Uruttiram Kannanar, Mamkudi Marutanar, and Kapilar.

But the names of the kings whose memory these princes of letters sought to embalm in their sweet verses are not, with perhaps a single exception, equally well-known to fame. The name of Karikala Chôla, in whose honour two of the ten Iyls are written, is of frequent occurrence in Tamil literature. It appears more than four times in *Kalingattu Parani*, a work that professes to celebrate a victory of Pallava Chôlas over the Kalingas, whose dominions seem to have stretched all along the eastern coast from Madras to the mouth of the

* [Pandit R. S. Vedachalam Pillai asserts that *Mullai-paddu* is dedicated to Nedumcheliyan, the hero of the succeeding two Idylls, *viz.*, *Madurai-Kanji* and *Nedunal-Vâdai*. *Vide* his short but excellent "Criticism on Mullaippaddu," in Tamil. Ed.]

Mahanady. Reference to Karikala is found in the *Skântham* which is subsequent only to the *Periya Puranam*. Flattering mention is also made of him in *Pala Moli*. He is again the subject of adulation in many verses cited as illustrations in *Tandi* and other grammatical treatises. Though his praises are thus widely sung, his coins and inscriptions, which would have been of greater service in modern researches, do not appear to have been equally numerous. At any rate epigraphists and numismatologists have not yet succeeded in fixing his age. Various and conflicting conjectures have, however, been started regarding it. Mr. Wilson assumes that he was the father of Mangaiarkkarasi, the famous queen of Kûn Pandia and the patroness of Sambanthar, but that apostle of Caiva has not a word to say of Karikala, from whose territories he must have come, if the hypothesis advanced has any truth in it. Mr. Taylor represents Karikâla as the last of the Chôlas and a mere protégé of the contemporary Pandia;—a character utterly inconsistent with the hero whose victories are so uniformly chanted by the poets of his age. Others charge him with the persecutions that Ramanuja Achariar suffered about the year 1117, while Dr. Caldwell with equal confidence places him in the thirteenth century. Inquiring into the age of the *Kural* and connecting it with the traditional account of its acceptance by the College Board at Madura, the venerable author observes, "If any weight could be attached to this tradition, it would bring down the *Kural* considerably, for other traditions connect Nakkîrar (who is always represented as the President of the College) with the reign of Karikâla Chôla who seems to have lived in the thirteenth century."* We are not aware of any tradition that directly connects Nakkîrar with Karikâla Chôla, but however that may be, it is simply preposterous to assign the thirteenth century to Nakkîrar, after placing Kamban in the twelfth, with the chance of being shifted to the tenth in accordance with the well-known stanza prefixed to his *Ramayana*. This is not the place for entering into any of the controversies

* Dr. Caldwell's *Comparative Dravidian Grammar*, p. 131.

to which these several conjectures have given rise. But we may nevertheless be permitted to make the remark that the discussion seems mainly to owe its origin to the fact of there having been, in more recent times, several Chôla princes who ruled under the honoured name of Karikâla—a source of confusion so common in Indian chronology. My friend Mr. Venkayya, the assistant epigraphist, (*now Epigraphist to the Government of India,*) tells me that he has heard of three Karikâla Chôlas, though nothing has yet been done to fix the age of any of them. This is just what one might expect. The first having been a remarkable warrior and administrator his name, or rather his nickname, (for the name Karikâla was given him only because he burned his foot through an accident) acted as a charm upon the people, and was assumed in consequence by several of his admiring successors.*

Since the names of the princes with whom the Idyls are associated afford no clue to determine their age, we have for the present to be content with such flickering rays of light as literature and purely literary traditions may throw on the subject. Taking then the best known of the eight authors of the Ten Idyls, *viz*.. Nakkîrar, let us see what literary traditions have to say about his age. In the first place, the orthodox pundits have no hesitation in placing him long before the age of Sambandhar, the great apostle of Caiva. In support of this universal impression of Tamil scholars such considerations as the following may be urged :—(1) There is such a difference in the style and the vocabulary of the two authors that scarcely any doubt can be entertained as to the long interval that must have separated the age of Nakkîrar from that of Sambandhar. (2) Nakkîrar is best known as the President of the Madura College, of which scarcely any trace seems to have existed at the time Sambandhar visited that ancient seat of learning. (3) Sambandhar's name is universally

* [The date of Karikala is fully discussed by Mr. S. Krishnaswamy Aiyengar, M.A., in the preceding article, "The Augustan Age of Tamil Literature." pp. 34, et seq. Ed.]

associated with the final downfall and disappearance of the Jains, while we find them flourshing in the days of Nakkîrar and his fellow pundits, who make very prominent mention, as we shall see further on, of their churches and associations. (4) Sundara, the last of the apostles of Çaiva, who is generally taken to have lived not long after Sambandhar, wrote a famous song entitled 'The Poets of true Piety', and all his expounders, from Nambi Andar Nambi downwards, agree in thinking that Nakkîrar is the poet chiefly referred to in that well-known hymn. (5) It is interesting to note that Nachinarkiniyar, the learned Caiva commentator, quotes not a line from Sambandhar in any of his elaborate annotations, while he scruples not to enforce his remarks by apt citations from Manikkavacagar, who, too, seems to have lived after the Madura College had become extinct. It is obvious, therefore, that in the days of Nachinarkiniyar, Sambandhar's usage had not become sufficiently old to be authoritative. (6) The Madura *Stala Purana*,* which though not strictly historical, cannot be said to be purely fictitious, mentions as many as twenty-six Pandiyas, between Vamsha Sêgara, in whose reign Nakkîrar is said to have flourished, and Kûn Pandiya, whom Sambandhar is claimed to have converted from Buddhism. This would leave an interval of at least four centuries, if we allow an average of fifteen years for each of the twenty-six Pandiyas.

For these reasons, we do not hesitate to conclude that Nakkîrar lived long prior to Sambandhar; and we shall probably be not far wrong if we estimate the interval between the two authors at three or four centuries.

Now if we can by any means ascertain the age of Sambandhar, that of Nakkîrar may be relatively fixed. It is well-known that Sambandhar converted Kûn Pandia from Buddhism, and so contributed to the final overthrow of that religion in Southern India. The question then is, when did Kûn Pandiya reign; and when was Buddhism finally over-

* See also Taylor's *Historical Manuscripts*, Vol. I. p. 23.

thrown? To neither of these questions, has archæology as yet given a satisfactory answer. Dr. Caldwell identifies Kûn Pandiya with a Sundara Pandia of certain inscriptions, and seeks to make out that Sundara Pandiya is none else than the Sender Bendi of Marco Polo, who flourished about the end of the thirteenth century. Mr. Nelson questions this conclusion, and rightly points out that as several princes ruled in Madura under the name of Sundara Pandiya subsequent to the days of Kûn Pandiya, more cogent reasons than those adduced by the author would be needed to support the identification of Kûn Pandiya with Marco Polo's Sender Bendi. For his own part, Mr. Nelson prefers to assign Kûn Pandiya to the latter half of the eleventh century. "Supposing therefore," he says, "that Ramanuja was persecuted by Karikâla, and that Mangaiarkarasai was the daughter of the latter, as alleged, it is very possible that Kûn Pandiya reigned in the latter half of the eleventh century." * We cannot but admire the caution with which this sentence is written, but we must nevertheless demur to the conclusion, based, as it is, upon highly questionable assumptions.

Turning then once more to literary traditions, we find Sankara Achariar, whose period Sanskrit scholars are now pretty nearly agreed in fixing in the eighth century, has a *sloka* in his *Soundarya Laharî*, in honour of Sambandhar, or the "Dravidian Infant of Parvathi," as he there calls him. This would indicate not only that Sambandhar flourished long before Sankara, but also that the interval of time that separated the two was sufficient to surround the memory of the former with a halo of divinity. Even allowing for the abnormal rapidity with which apotheosis develops in tropical India, we cannot accept any interval less than two or three centuries as enough for a philosopher of Sankara's wide experience and well-known acuteness, to be led to its acceptance. It must be further remembered that Sankara differed largely from Sambandhar in his ultimate religious views, and

* Nelson's *Manual of the Madura Country*, Part III. Chapter ii. p. 65.

was really a stranger to the Tamil people, since he won his fame chiefly in Upper India, and by writings that are entirely in Sanskrit.

Now if *Soundarya Luhuri* is accepted as a genuine production of Sankara Achariar, and it must be so assumed until very substantial reasons are shown to the contrary, the age of Sambanthar cannot but be earlier than the period of Sankara. The Hon'ble Mr. Justice Telang * adduces certain sound reasons for placing that period in the sixth century; but for our purposes, it is enough to assume the age usually assigned to him, *viz.*, the eighth century. Allowing, then, an interval of two centuries, we arrive at the sixth century as the probable era of Sambandhar.

That we are not claiming too high an antiquity for Sambandhar, and that if there be any error at all, the error is on the other side, will be evident from such facts as the following. In the first place, the pious Buddhist traveller, Hiuen Tsiang, who spent nearly sixteen years, from 629 to 645 A. D., in visiting all the provinces of India, and in studying the prospects of his religion in its birth-place, does not give any flattering report of Buddhism in the Tamil countries. Neither in Chôla nor in Malakûta, which Dr. Burnell identifies with the delta of the Kavêry river, does he note any remarkable Buddhist institution. To him the people of the former land "are dissolute and cruel," while those of the latter are "not fond of learning but wholly given to commercial pursuits." Hiuen Tsiang does not appear to have visited Madura at all,—an omission altogether unaccountable, had it been still the stronghold of Buddhism that it was before the days of Sambandhar. In all probability, the Chinese traveller came into the Tamil provinces only after Caivaism under Sambandhar had triumphantly overthrown the religion of Buddha.†

---

* See the *Indian Antiquary,* Vol. xiii. p. 95. According to Mr. J. F Fleet, Sankara lived about 630—655 A. D. *Ibid.*, Vol. xvi. p. 41.

† [Tradition as well as the *Stala-puranas* of Madura say that Kûn Pandian was converted from Jainism and the state religion was then Jainism and not Buddhism. It is also said that after the conversion of Pandian to

Again Sundara—the author of the hymn which celebrates the sixty-three Caiva saints, including Sambandhar—was the companion of that Cheraman Perumal who is said to have so mysteriously disappeared from his country. Though the orthodox pundits are adverse to any identification of this pious Cheraman with the last of the Perumals, yet the similarity in the accounts given of the two is too strong to be accidental. But if there be any error at all in this identification, it would be once more only an error on the side of moderation. Assuming then that the Chera friend of Sundara was the last of the Perumals, we cannot but suppose that Sundara lived in the early part of the eighth century, the age usually claimed for the last of the Perumals. This accords well also with the local tradition in Malabar, which connects the *Kollam* era, with the destruction of a port called Kollam, subsequent to the flight of the last of the Perumals. That Sundara belonged to the earlier part of the century may be further inferred from the fact that, while he names several minor contemporary saints in his famous hymn, he has not a word to say of Sankara, who so thoroughly revolutionized the religion of his country. Now if Sundara lived in the early years of the *eighth century*, we have to assign to Sambandhar a period two or three centuries earlier. Such an interval alone can account for the reverence with which the former names the latter, and for the fact, that while Sambandhar's career met everywhere with stout opposition from the Buddhists, not one single anecdote has come down to us of such resistance to Sundara.

Caivism, Sambandha caused the death of 8000 Jains who were persistent in their faith. Thus Jainism was rooted out from the Pandia country in the 7th cent. A. D. and this is pointed out by Sundaram Pillai himself when he says "Sambandhar's name is universally associated with the final downfall and disappearence of the Jains;" but he, in subsequent pages, confounds Jainism with Buddhism. Buddhism was introduced into South India and Ceylon by Asoka in the 3rd cent. B. C. We see its ascendency in the Tamil land, from the post-Sangam works, in the early centuries of the Christian era. About the 4th cent. A. D. Buddhism was overthrown by the great Caiva saint Manikkavacagar and it began to decline. In the 5th cent. Fa Hian, the Chinese traveller in India, saw the signs of the declension of his religion in the South. Two centuries subsequent when Hiuen Tsiang visited India, he went as far as Kanji but returned from there as he saw that Buddhism had already been swept away from the Pandia and Chola countries. Thus it will be seen that the religious struggle in the 7th cent. was not between Buddhism and Caivism but between Caivism and Jainism. Ed.]

The third circumstance we would mention would settle the era of Sambandhar beyond all question, if only its truth could be fully ascertained. The present honoured head of the *Sambandha Muttam* at Madura claims to be the 114th in succession from the original apostle,* and if this assertion is true, we should reach very close to the fifth century, even allowing but twelve years for each of the deceased 113 representatives of the monastery.

On these grounds, we think it not unreasonable to assume that Sambandhar lived about the fifth century. At any rate, with the evidence before us, it is impossible to assign to him a period later than the seventh century.† We may therefore take the fifth and seventh centuries as marking the limits of his probable age. Now if Nakkîrar, as already shown, lived two or three centuries before Sambanthar, it would follow that the age of our poet cannot be later than the fifth century, while it is quite possible that he lived two or three centuries earlier.

But the age of Nakkîrar is not the age of all the Ten Idyls. Probably most of them were in existence in his days. The allegorical use he makes of the form of poetic composition, known as *âttuppadai*, would itself argue the later origin of his work. His *âttuppadai* is most likely the last of the kind, and the collection of the Ten Idyls was perhaps made in his own time. We may therefore *tentatively* place the composition of the book of Idyls about the beginning of the Christian era.

Now passing to the poems themselves, we may note that five of the Idyls are of that form of poetic composition called

---

* Damodaram Pillai's *Vîrachôlham*, p. 17. According to Mr. Nelson, the present head is the 277th hereditary manager. Evidently the records of the *Muttam* must be imperfect when two such different results can be derived from them.

† [Prof. Sundaram Pillai has, on further research, assigned the opening of the 7th cent. A. D., as the date to Sambandha, in his work entitled "Some mile-stones in the History of Tamil Literature." And Rai Bahadur V. Venkayya, in his *Introduction* to the Professor's work, suggests that, as the destruction of Vadapi took place probably in A. D. 642, the middle of the century might be the date. See *the Tamilian Antiquary*, No. 3. Ed.]

âttuppadai, which, under the pretext of guiding a needy traveller to an open-handed and bountiful prince, describes in flattering terms the provinces and cities of the latter, and his prowess and position. It is generally put as if addressed by a minstrel, songster, or actor, who returns well loaded with presents from a generous prince, to a fellow minstrel, songster, or actor in search of a patron. Except the first, which is dedicated to the war god Muruga, the remaining four literally fulfil this description. The first named, 'The Guide to Muruga,' adopts this usual form of address to chant the praise of that god and to direct the pious-minded to his worship. This figurative and curious use of the original convention is noteworthy, as it helps to indicate the relative age of the works under consideration. Nakkîrar could not have thought of making an allegorical use of this form of address, if he had not had several instances of the literal kind before him; and it is possible that some of the very works here grouped with his may have been the models from which he copied. Of the remaining five Idyls, four are erotic, *viz.*, the 5th, 7th, 8th and 9th; while the central idea of the sixth, or *Maduraikkânchi* is to direct attention to a world beyond the present.

But as in the case of all Idyls, it is not so much the central idea or purpose that is of interest, as the imagery in which it is set, and the description of nature for which it serves as an occasion. 'The Guide to Muruga,' the first of the Idyls, is certainly not the best, though it happens to be the only one now generally known to the public. In the general wreck of letters that followed the extinction of the Madura College, Muruga's name seems to have served as a life-boat to this work of Nakkîrar and to have saved it from that undeserved oblivion which overwhelmed its more illustrious compeers. It forms along with nine other minor works of Nakkîrar a portion of the Eleventh Collection of the sacred hymns of the Caivas, and with the devotees of Muruga, it is a part of their daily liturgy. A miraculous story is told of the occasion that gave birth to this work. It is said that a certain giant was in the habit of dining upon one thousand men at a time, and that on a particular day, as only nine hundred and ninety-nine were ready, Nakkîrar was caught and added to the lot to make up the requisite number. But the mathematical giant was also somewhat puritanical, and so, after completing the number, instead of sitting down at once to breakfast, he foolishly went to perform his daily ablutions and thus afforded time for Nakkîrar to compose the poem in praise of Muruga, who, moved by its pathos, appeared at once on the spot, killed the fastidious giant and released the poet and his nine hundred and ninety-nine fellow prisoners.

Whatever may be its supernatural virtues, 'The Guide to Muruga' is from a literary point of view inferior to many of its companion Idyls, and decidedly so to Nakkîrar's own *Nedunalvâdai*. It begins with a description of the delicate mountain fairies that go about dancing and singing in praise of Muruga's victories, and the fantastic furies, that with ears large enough for owls and serpents to sleep in, take delight in plucking out and eating the eyeballs of those slain in his battles. The poet then goes on to direct those who wish to abstract their attention from worldly concerns and to fix it on Muruga, to seek him in certain favoured places. The first of these is Thirupparamkunram, the hill in the vicinity of Madura,—the next railway station in fact on the way from Madura to Tinnevelly. It is described by the poet as west of Madura, though the hill is really to the south-west of the modern town. Madura is alluded to in glorious words, and reference is made to the ancient manner of indicating an impregnable fortress. "At the gates of Madura," says the poet, "is hoisted the flag of victory, and by its side sleeps the image of a girl with a leather-ball in her hands." The image was hung up to represent the enemies and as a challenge to them to approach the fortress. The place next mentioned is Thiruchîralavây, which is now identified with Thiruchentoor. In this connection, the six faces and the twelve hands of Muruga with their occupations are described in vivid terms. The third place mentioned is Thiruvâvin Nan Kudi. The commentator remarks that this is the ancient name of the place, which in the days of Avvaiyar came to be called Chittanvâlvu,—a testimony of great value as showing the long interval that must have elapsed between Nakkîrar and Avvaiyar, who is reckoned by Dr. Caldwell himself as a contemporary of Kamban, and is placed therefore in the twelfth century.* Here Muruga is said to hold a levee of all the gods and saints, which we may suspect to indicate a procession on ceremonial occasions. At any rate, the description of the emaciated saints with their saffron-coloured cloths and deer skins is suggestive of an earthly rather than of a heavenly scene. Avvaiyar also alludes to the place as a village remarkable for Brahmin piety. The place next noticed, *viz.*, Thiruvêragam, seems to have been an equally famous Brahmin colony. The Brahmins are described as uttering their prayers after their ablutions, and with wet cloths on their bodies,—a habit still noticeable in villages on the banks of the Kâvêry and the Tambrapûrani. Of course, no example of the rule, here extolled, of devoting the first forty-eight years of one's life to the study of the Vedas, can be now anywhere found. Thiruvêragam † is generally identified with a village near Kumbaconam, though the commentator speaks of it as a village in the hilly districts,—a description not in the least applicable to the country about Kumbaconam. The poet then speaks of Muruga as taking a part in the festive dances of the mountaineers, clad in the green leaves of the forests. No particular place is here specified, but every hill is mentioned as the scene of such joyous mingling of gods and men.

But the concluding passage of the work is, perhaps, the best. It reveals some of the curious habits of the people of

* [There were two poetesses known by the name of Avvaiyar. The first was the Avvaiyar of the Sangam age who was brought up by a Pana family and who claimed a brotherhood with the sage Tiruvalluvar. Her poems are found in the "Eight Collections" of the last Sangam. The second one was—*the woman who did*—a self made woman unmarried, belonging to a Vaniya family of Uraiur, who came forward in her older age and was honoured by the name of Avvai. She was the contemporary of Kamban -the poet. Ed.]

† [Eragam is a place in the Western Ghats in the District of Madura. Ed.]

those ancient times, which are not yet altogether extinct. The sacrifice of goats on festive occasions, the hypnotic dances which accompany such festivities, the sacred groves and junctions of three or four streets, the spreading tree under which the village elders meet for transacting public business, the stones planted in pastures for cows to rub themselves against, are all mentioned as tempting situations for meeting Muruga; and most of these are still matters of interest in the out-of-the-way villages. The scene of the sacrifice is painted in detail, and it requires but little effort to identify many of the particulars with those which occur even to this day in remote rustic parts. A shed is put up with garlands of equal length hanging on all sides. A flag is hoisted with the head of a man and the body of a bird to frighten off unwelcome devils. The officiating priest wears a double set of cloths, mutters mantras, and begins the ceremonies with bending and raising the upper part of his body a certain number of times, having his hands so crossed as to touch his ears. He has a thread tied round his wrist, scatters flowers and fried paddy on all sides, kills a bull (according to the annotator it is only a goat,) and then, mingling with its blood rice and a little turmeric powder, offers the morsel with sweetmeats of different preparations to Muruga. With the burning of incense, an awful devil dance ensues, in the course of which the priest (or rather the priestess as it happens to be in this particular case) declares to the worshippers an indemnity from famine, epidemics, and war. In the hilly tracts of Travancore, such scenes are not at all rare, and the class of people who officiate at these ceremonies are still called Vêlan,—the very term used in the text. The poem closes by assuring the pious traveller of the favour of the deity, if the seeker after Muruga goes to any one of these places and duly worships him. There is nothing in the text or in the commentary to show that the hills described in the closing lines of the poem are the Pulney hills, though popularly supposed to be so, in order to make up the six camps of the war god, as they are enumerated at present. The poem, however, names only four particular spots sacred to that deity.

Such is the outline of the first of the Idyls, which is by no means the best of them. A glance at the poem will show how antiquated the style is. We will just mention but one or two of the archaisms with which the work abounds. One of the suffixes for forming the past participle from a verb is 'pu'; but it is so seldom used that even Kamban, in the very preface to his immortal *Ramayana* makes a blunder with it, using it as an infinitive instead of as the past participle. 'Nakkupu' means 'having licked' and not 'to lick' as Kamban would have it to mean. Now in Nakkîrar's poem under notice, which contains but 317 lines in all, this suffix is used eleven times, and that in connections where there is not the least difficulty, metrical or other, to justify the use of this rare form. Again, the repetition and elongation of the final vowel sound of a verb, called *alapedai*, to indicate the past participle, is but rarely resorted to in modern literature: but in the 317 lines of this poem it occurs thirty times. I shall not, however, try the patience of the general reader by going into such grammatical details. Turning then to the vocabulary of the poem, we find but thirty Sanskrit words, even counting such common words as தாமரை (lotus), மனம் (mind), and மீன் (fish), as well as words so far altered and Dravidianized as முத்து (pearl), and உலகம் (world). Taking each line to have an average of five words the 317 lines of the poem do not show two per cent. of Sanskrit words. It may be interesting also to notice that even the ancient commentator, Nachinârkkiniyar, finds it necessary to point out different readings in the poem, in three or four connections, showing how long the work must have existed even before his days. The Puranic account of the birth of Muruga, as given by the commentator, differs in certain important particulars from the account now generally accepted. It seems not altogether impossible that Muruga was originally a Dravidian deity; and that in the course of time, when Aryan civilization found it expedient to adopt the cult of the independent nations over which it came to exercise its influence, a place in the Puranic mythology was found for the war god of the Tamils, as transformed and embellished by Aryan genius, just as in more recent times, Buddhistic institutions and even Buddha himself, under the name of Sasta,* came to be absorbed into Brahminism.

But we have tarried too long over the first of the Idyls, which as we have more than once remarked, is certainly not the best of the collection. We therefore pass at once to the *Nedunalvâdai* of Nakkîrar, the seventh in the collection of Idyls, promising to return to the intermediate ones in due course. Unlike 'The Guide to Muruga,' *Nedunalvâdai* or 'The Dreary Winter' is confined to purely mundane matters. It is written in honour of a king of Madura who passed under the name of Nedunchelyan, the hero of Thalaiálangâ-nam. Nothing is now positively known of this Pandia or of the victory with which his name is associated. His name does not find a place in any known list of Pandiyas, Puranic or other. At first sight it may be doubted whether it is a proper name at all · Cheliyan is but one of the many synonyms of Pandiyas, meaning literally the prosperous, and Nedu, meaning tall or great, seems to be but a honorific prefix. Probably the poets at the court of this Prince familiarly spoke of him by this soubriquet, exactly as the courtiers of Edward I. knew him as Longshanks. According to the *Stala Purana* of Madura, the Pandiyan who reigned in the time of Nakkîrar was one *Vamsa Ségara.* But no recollection of his military glories seems to have survived at the time when that *Purana* was composed. But as the function of the *Stala Purana* is to relate only such occurrences as illustrate the *Lîlas*, or the sacred amusements of the presiding deity of the city, no conclusion can be drawn from its silence on this point. Among the eulogies pronounced on the *Kural* when it was accepted by the College Board, there is a stanza attributed to Ukkira Peru Valutiyar, presumably the then king of Madura. May not Peru Valutiyar, be the same as Neduncheliyan? Both names convey the same idea—the great Pandiya. But we

---

* Sasta means literally a teacher, and, according to Amara, the word is but a synonym for Buddha.

leave such speculations to those who have the leisure and means for conducting them.*

Confining ourselves to the work in hand, we have every reason to believe that the patron of Nakkîrar, whoever he was, was a powerful sovereign in his day, who by his indefatigable energy and indomitable valour won undying laurels for himself, and honour for his country. *Far and near, he was a terror to his enemies.* Vâna Viral Vêl was dispossessed of his capital,—the flourshing town of Alumbil—because he was slow to acknowledge his allegiance to Nedunchelian. The thriving ports of Muthuvillil and Nelloor † were captured in no time. The princes of Kuttanad—a portion of Travancore east of the modern town of Alleppey—were among those who felt his prowess and wisely owned his sway to escape destruction. But it is his glorious victory at Thalai Alanganam that is universally associated with his name. If we are to believe Nachinarkkiniyar this victory was won against great odds. Two sovereigns like himself, Chera and Chola, and five feudatory princes, named Thitian, Eluni, Erumaiyûran, Irumgovonman, and Porunan, seem to have made a combined effort to crush this Napoleon of ancient Madura, but all in vain. "Even their drums," says the author of *Madurai Kanji*, "were captured in this field of military Yaga or sacrifice to the Gods." A glorious description of this battle is found also in *Purrappâttu* a rare classical work of great antiquity. It is impossible to doubt, with these facts before us, that Thalai Alanganam was the scene of a decisive victory, which at once raised the prestige of the Madura Country and stirred up the literary activity of its people. In all probability, Alanganam bore the same relation to the age of Nakkîrar

---

* [Mr. S. Krishnasawmy Aiyengar adduces proofs to identify Nedun-cheliyan with Ugra-Pandiyan. *Vide* his article on the "Augustan age of Tamil Literature" pp. 40 & 41. We accept this and are further of opinion that this Neduncheliyan who was a very powerful warrior and was known as the 'terror to his enemies' is the "Kadum-Kôn" of the last Sangam. Kadum Kôn and Ugra Pandian are synonymous terms. Ed.]

† Can this be the modern town Nelloor? The commentator is inclined to identify it with Saliyûr a town of his own times. [Sali is synonymous to nel=paddy.]

and his College, that the defeat of the Armada bore to the Elizabethan era of English letters. When more of the real history of these ancient times comes to be known, Alamkanam and the M .Jura College will be found to afford but another illustration of the well established induction that links the literary progress of a nation with its political pre-eminence. But whether more of the history of the age is likely to be known or not, this much is beyond question, that the hero of A'langanam was a restless warrior of the times, and that he had certainly more stern duties to perform than offering prizes for poems on the tresses of his lady-love, as the *Stala Purana* would have it. The poem of Nakkirar under notice itself bears ample testimony in this respect. It is in fact a prayer for the king's safe and quick return to the bosom of his queen, who passes restless nights in silent tears, because of the absence of her lord on the battle field.

It is one of these nights that the poet here undertakes to depict. The scene is laid in the bed-chambers of the palace; but the poet approaches it from the far off rural parts, to which the shepherds have removed their cattle with the first appearance of the monsoon. It is now the end of November, and the heavy clouds, having exhausted their first fury, are now practising, as the poet puts it, the gentler art of drizzling. But the weather continues cold, and the howling north winds are all the more fierce. The monkey on the tree shivers and contracts its limbs, and having given up its arboreal marches and depredations, now looks small indeed! The birds overborne by the winds drop down in their flights: but they still make way as best as they can, to the shoals and shallow parts of the rivers, to which the fishes, unable to withstand the unusually strong currents, repair in crowds; and once there, the winged visitors make but short work of their aquatic friends. The milch cows shivering with cold forget their motherly affections, and instead of welcoming their calves, drive them off with a kick. The shepherds fare even worse. This is not the time for them to gather their favourite flowers or to indulge in their other pastoral amusements.

They are now far from their homes, and the nights are specially trying to them. Exposed to the moaning piercing winds, they collect in small companies of twos and threes, and light up their fires, which make but darkness visible, exactly as their small companies make their solitude all the more impressive and pronounced. They warm the palms of their hands at these fires, and applying them to their cheeks, seek to persuade their teeth from chattering and 'drumming' (as the saying in Tamil runs) against each other. From these rural parts the poet leads us to the city through fertile paddy-fields, elegant arecanut groves, and orchards adorned with different flowers. The ripening paddy ears bow in prayer; the elongated tender arecanuts are becoming rounder with the ingathering of the fragrant catechu for which they are prized, and the boughs of the orchard trees, dripping occasional tear drops, kiss one another overhead.

It is evening when we enter the town; and passing through the streets which are as broad as rivers, we meet with strong-bodied, sinewy, Mlachas, clad in loose garments, moving to and fro, full-drunk, and therefore unmindfull of rain and winds. We should like to become better acquainted with these drunken foreigners,—particulary with regard to their nationality—but the poet vouchsafes no further information. Meantime the fair ladies of the houses on both sides of the streets, inferring the advent of night from the opening of the *pichi* (jasmine) buds in their flower-baskets, light up their iron lamps, and scattering paddy and flowers on all sides perform their evening worship. The domesticated pigeons, however, have no such means of inference, and failing to distinguish day from night, they simply alter their posture and exchange seats with their lovely mates, in the way of relieving the monotony of their enforced idleness. The menials, we observe, are engaged in grinding and preparing musk perfumes on small stones "as hard and polished as the surface of gram." For sandal paste, so unsuitable for the cold season, is nowhere in demand. For the same reason, garlands are also not in favour. The small-mouthed cold water jugs are not now in use. The exquisitely wrought fan, again, hangs in a corner, covered with cobwebs. The fire-pan and the smoke-pan are, on the contrary, everywhere in requisition. To the ordinary incenses burned in the latter, a small quantity of molasses is added in conformity with medical directions to keep off cold and catarrh. As we pass, we notice that the windows are all closed against the wind, and the airy bed-chambers in the second storey are almost forsaken. Women given to dancing now take to singing, and to keep the strings of their harps at a proper temperature, they rub them frequently against their warm bosoms.

By this time we have reached the tower gates of the palace, which look like tunnels worked through mountains, but are yet high enough not to obstruct the royal standard carried erect on the royal elephant's back. The strong doors are models of architectural skill and beauty, and are so well fitted that not even smoke can pass through. But through the favour of the poet we succeed in finding a passage, and are now in the courtyard of the palace. It is thickly strewn with white sand, and is intended for the mirth-ful sports of the musk-deer and other rare animals brought up in the royal residence. But just now melancholy silence reigns there, broken only by the occasional neighing of the overfed and underworked horses in the stables, the monotonous flow of rain water from the catchpipes of the terraces of the palace, and the infrequent but awful cawing of the peacock in the royal aviary. Entering the palace, we pass through long corridors lit up by lamps borne by images of Yavana manufacture. Of these Yavanas, too, we are curious to know some particulars, but the poet hurries us through several spacious and well-lighted rooms to the zenanas, which he stays minutely to describe. These buildings are as high as mountains, and the flags that adorn them are as varied in colour as the rainbow. Into this unapproachable compartment,—unapproachable, it is said, to every male human being except the king—the poet fearlessly leads us, and takes us direct to the royal bedroom.

There is in that bedroom an ivory cot, well curtained, painted and ornamented and cushionêd ; but to reproduce in English the poet's minute description of it would require Sir Walter Scott's command of descriptive terminology and his genius for details. As moreover this notice is intended to invite and not to supersede a careful study of the original, we may pass over such minutiæ. Well ; the poet then points to us a lady lying on that cot, with eyes wide open, but so absorbed in melancholy reflection that probably she would not note our presence in that forbidden place even if we were bodily there. No ornaments now adorn her natural beauty ; not even a pearl necklace is there to keep company with the sacred marriage thread loosely lying on her bosom. A pair of tiny ear-rings now does duty for the wonted priceless ear-pendants. On her forearms we notice the mark left by golden bracelets, but their place is now occupied by poor conchshell wristlets. A solitary *mudakka* or *nalivu* (as it is now generally called) guards the slender fingers that usually wear but the finest of rings. Her angelic form is now clad, not in silk, but in ordinary cotton fabrics. Thus like an outline picture waiting to be coloured, lies the queen, sleepless and careworn ; and it must be remembered that it was midnight when we entered the royal bedchamber. As she rolls her eyes in thoughtless abstraction, she notices on the curtains of the cot a picture of the heavenly bodies ; and the scene recalls to her the preferential love that the moon so notoriously entertains for Rohini,* and all further vision is obstructed by the flow of tears. In such distress, then lies the queen. But where is the king ?

In answer to this question the poet takes us a long way out of the country. The king is in foreign lands, wintering in his camp for the rainy season. But is he there sleeping in a snug corner of his camp in the dead of this selfsame night ? No ! Is he also love sick and restless ? Far from it ! He is

* Rohini is a group of stars in Taurus, said to be the favourite queen of the moon, and on that account an object of jealousy with every other of the 7 groups of stars.

too busy for that! If we follow our poet and go into the camp, we may see him this very hour, moving from quarter to quarter, visiting the wounded and comforting the sick. Lo! you see him walking under an umbrella and behind a torch, whose light is flaming at right angles to its handle, because of the steady northern wind, so fierce and piercing. By his side is the general of his forces, pointing out one by one the heroes of previous day's skirmish, and also the wounds that mark their valour. There, as he passes by the stables, you may note how the horses, standing day and night saddled and ready for battle, neigh and shake off the water drops from their sturdy sides, as if indicating their preparedness for immediate action. Nor is the king less prepared. For, behold his royal sword is carried by his trusted *aide-de-camp*, on whose broad shoulders the king familiarly reposes his right hand! Warriors know no distinction among mankind, but that of the brave and the coward! Well! we have now seen how the king and his queen spend this dreary rainy night; and having witnessed the two scenes, who among us would not join the poet in heartily wishing a glorious termination to the war and a speedy return of the monarch to the bosom of his beloved wife?

Such is the outline of Nakkirar's *Nedunalvâdai*; and I would request the reader to study it in the original, and then to say whether the author does not deserve to be placed among the very best of the poets of any country. The extreme simplicity of the central conception, the natural ease with which it is developed, the pleasing but in every way true and accurate portraits of nature amid which it is set, and the taste and tact with which every line is made to subserve the one single artistic effect that the whole piece is intended to produce, are simply admirable. It is only after carefully studying this remarkable production of Nakkirar that one is able to understand and appreciate the universal voice of antiquity that declares Nakkirar the prince and president of the Madura College of Pundits. It is only then, that the old story of Nakkirar's venturesome criticism on the verse of Civa, the terrible deity of Madura, reveals any meaning. The story, I hope, is well known to the general reader. The reigning Pandia of Madura, having discovered a natural fragrance in the tresses of his queen, promised a rich reward—a lump of gold—to any poet that would tell him what thought he had in his mind. The poets of the College essayed in turn, but none succeeded in solving this Rosicrucian puzzle. A poor ignorant Brahmin devotee of Civa saw in the juncture a fine opportunity for pocketing the gold, and completing the matrimonial arrangements he had then in contemplation. He appeared accordingly before the local deity and prayed to be put in possession of the valuable information. The deity, who of course knew what queer thought had passed in the mind of the prince, granted the supplication, and favoured his dependent with a stanza praising the natural fragrance of the queen's hair. On the production of the lines, the gold was at once ordered to be awarded; but the jealous pundits, writhing under discomfiture, interposed. The stanza was produced before the president of their College, our Nakkirar, who at once condemned it on the score of the fantastic idea it conveyed. No human hair, whether queen's or king's, said our poet, could have any odour that was not artificial or accidental. The Brahmin ignoramus was, of course, unable to reply to the criticism; and he therefore ran again for help to his deity, who now felt himself in honour bound to defend his production. He appeared accordingly in the guise of an old Brahmin, and attempted a defence; but being soon driven into a corner, the deity sought to ensnare his adversary by 'special pleadings,' and asked him whether his proposition would apply to the hair of the goddess of Madura, of whom the poet was a special devotee. All undaunted, Nakkîrar would admit no exception to his proposition; and it proved too much for the patience of the god. Already irritated by opposition, he was now touched to the quick by the insult offered to the goddess, his better half. Off went his disguise, and with his third eye that opens only to burn up the universe, fast simmering and smouldering with fire, the angry deity commanded Nakkîrar to retract the offensive criticism. But neither for god nor for man would our poet flinch from truth; and though death stared him in the face, he declined to countenance the unnatural conceit conveyed by the poem. The terrible third eye of Civa was now opened in full, and to escape the fierce fire that ensued, Nakkirar and his College of fellow Pundits, the story concludes,* had to take refuge in the Lotus Tank within the local temple. So did might triump over right! But what is the meaning of this tradition,—almost the only one that has come down to us of Nakkirar? Does it not point to the extreme realism in his style? Does it not show that the poet's love of truth, love of nature, was so strong, so unswerving that he would defy all authorities, human and divine, for the sake of maintaining accuracy of representation, truthfulness of thought, even in poetic composition? I take the whole story as the best panegyric that can be pronounced on the poet's love of nature and his unconquerable hatred of all kinds of extravagance in thought or expression: and no praise in that line will be ever found too much for the author of *Nedunalvâdai.*

P. SUNDRAM PILLAY.

---

* Sivaprakasar slightly tampers with this story to suit his own purposes. See his *Kalatti Purana*; *Nakktra-Charukam.*

Dravidian Kingdoms.*

BY

Dewan Bahadur T. M. Rengachariar, B.A., B.L.,

AND

Mr. T. Desikachariar, B.A.. B.L.,

In ancient times the extreme south of India from the modern Tripati to Cape Comorin was split up into various small divisions, each under a petty chieftain but all acknowledging the suzerainty of one or other of the three great Dravidian Powers known to tradition as the Muvarasar (lit. three Kings.) Predominant among these was the Pandiya whose borders fluctuated with the martial powers of the ruling prince for the time being, but were under normal conditions pretty much as a Tamil Poetess set them down in verses which bear the following translation. "South of the river Vellar, Comorin on the south, the ocean loved of the wild seagull on the east with the great plain on the west." The tract of country comprised within these boundaries corresponds to the present Madura and Tinnevelly Districts and a good portion of the District of Trichinopoly, thus forming the southernmost portion of the Presidency of Madras. Compared with the extent of the Empire of the Great Buddhist Emperor Asoka in the 3rd Century B. C. this South Indian Province sinks into the level of a principality of very modest dimensions. But the great *Priyadarsin* himself recognised the Pandiyas as independent monarchs and their country as a neighbouring realm. Ptolemy in his geography and the unknown author of the Periplur both refer to the Pandiyan Kingdom as prosperous and independent powers in the south of India.

Along with the sister Dravidian Kingdoms the Pandiyan country, by its peculiar geographical position was rendered immune from attacks from the Kings who ruled north of the

* A reprint from the Wednesday Review, Trichinopoly.

Vindhiya range, an immunity enjoyed till the momentous era of the advent of the Muhammadan arms into the south of India in the beginning of the 14th Century A.D. Even so late as in the 13th Century A. D. Marco Polo declared the country of the Pandya as the "finest and noblest" where were found "very great pearls." To such an extent were the wealth and importance born of foreign commercial intercourse developed, that in the early centuries of the Christian era *Yavana* (Roman or Greek) mercenaries were tempted to serve under the Pandiyan Fish Banner and mount guard on the lofty towers of his Capital Madura. And judging from Numismatic evidence it is equally certain that in the flourishing periods of the Roman Empire there was a colony of Roman merchants settled on the banks of the Vaigai.

The name *Pandiya* is referred to in the *Vârtikas* of Katyayana, a sage who probably flourished in the 4th Century B.C. The hero of the great epic Ramayana, counted on the assistance of a Pandiya in his search for Sita, Kalidasa's Raghuvamsa has a description of a tour of conquest made by Raghu, the great grand-father of Rama, to whom the Pandiyan King rendered homage by gems collected from the oceanbed where the Tamraparni rolled its waves.

The antiquity of the Dravidian Kingdoms is attested to also by references to them in ancient Tamil literature. The finest and by far the most original Tamil works have been, for various reasons ascribed to the age of the third and last sangam "the far-famed College of Poets" which had its sittings at Madura, probably about the 1st Century A. D. These works throw a flood of light on the political history and civilisation of the country nearly 2,000 years ago. A highly developed monarchical Government aided by popular assemblies is assumed by them to have been the heritage of ages. The arts of peace no less than of war seem to have been assiduously cultivated and glowing descriptions abound of richly laden merchantmen visiting the emporiums on the East and West Coasts of the Dravida country. The Pandiyans, who were great patrons of literature, treated their pandits and poets with consideration and rewarded them with liberality. All this must have had behind it centuries of gradual and steady progress thus furnishing another indication of the extreme antiquity of the Dravidian Kingdom.

The same conclusion is pointed to by references contained in the early chronicles of Ceylon. Sinhalese traditions make it out that the founder of the "Mahavamso," great Dynasty, married a Pandiyan Princess and styled himself Panduvamsa Deva. Many an interesting episode in the Ceylon Chronicle deals with the attempted invasion of the island by the Pandiyan and consequent reprisals on the mainland by the Sinhalese Monarch. More than once in the 2nd Century A. D. the Tamils of Madura overran the north of Ceylon and remained for some years in possession of Anuradhapura, an achievement which bears testimony to the degree of military organisation, of which the Pandiyan power was at that early period capable.

For about the first ten centuries of the Christian era the central tableland of India south of the Vindhiya Mountains was the scene of a constant struggle for power, each dynasty succeeding to pre-eminence for a time only to give place to a successful rival. During all this period the Pandiyan ruled in the Tamil country apparently with the same prosperity as in the times of Asoka and Ptolemy. The province described by Hiouen Thsang, in the 7th Century A. D. as bounded on the south by the sea, and on the north by the Dravidian Kingdom with its capital Kanchipuram, and abounding with mountains in which grew the Sandal and Camphor trees was probably no other than that of the Pandiyas which under the prosperous rule of Kun Pandya was of no inconsiderable importance. So late as the 13th Century A. D. the Venetian Traveller, Marco Polo, refers to the five Pandiyan Kingdoms as the best of all the Indies, while the Muhammadan historians of the same period describe the Pandiyan country as 'Malabar' and the key of Hind in which Sundar Pandi and his brothers obtained power in different directions.

A Dravidian Kingdom which from all accounts was in a flourishing condition for nearly twenty centuries has yet no reliable connected chronicle of the doings of its Kings. Ancient Tamil Poetry concerned itself more with the true course of love and the rare excellence of the path of the "th aw" and virtue and the dire retribution of Nemeses tha with history and chronology. The oldest literature extant no doubt refers to the doings of the Dravida Kings who ruled about the age of the last Madura College of Poets, but it must be remembered that even these doings were recounted by bards in language naturally embellished by poetical imagery and influenced by a sense of grateful appreciacion of their patron's liberality.

Works composed with an avowedly religious object could obviously neither further nor aid historic investigation, unless the accounts contained in them were corroborated by evidence gleaned from independent sources. Such are the Periyapuranam of Sekkilar composed for the illustration of the lives of the sixty-three Caiva Saints, and the Tiruvilayâdal of Paranjoti, dealing primarily with the sporting feats of Civa as Sundareswara.

Some useful guidance is no doubt furnished by the poetry of a later age, but that is a period, for unravelling whose history we have the help of more unerring guides, viz, the numerous inscriptions with which the Tamil country was flooded to commemorate the gifts to Temples and religious uses made by pious sovereigns during the Chola ascendancy in South India. It is not a little disconcerting to the historical enquirer to be compelled to appeal to such uncertain source- for building the history and chronology of a race of Kings who were so great and adventurous as to have been in a posis tion to send an embassy to Augustus, invade Ceylon and rule over probably one of the earliest civilised communities in India for a longer period than any other monarchy. We will trace in a latter issue the origin of this ancient Kingdom.